To Devon,
& Charlie

Be lucky

[signature]

# Credit Derivatives:
# Applications for Risk Management

# Credit Derivatives:
# Applications for Risk Management

Published by Euromoney Books
in association with
Barclays Capital
Helaba Landesbank Hessen-Thüringen
PricewaterhouseCoopers

Published by
Euromoney Publications PLC
Nestor House, Playhouse Yard
London EC4V 5EX

Telephone: +44 (71) 779 8888

Copyright © 1998 Euromoney Publications PLC
ISBN 1 85564 639 0

This publication is not included in the CLA Licence so do not copy without the permission of the publisher.

All rights reserved. No part of this publication may be reproduced or used in any form (graphic, electronic or mechanical, including photocopying, recording, taping or information storage and retrieval systems) without permission by the publisher.

The views and opinions expressed in the book are solely those of the authors and need not necessarily reflect those of the institutions which have acted as co-publishers to the book. Although Euromoney has made every effort to ensure the complete accuracy of the text, neither it nor the authors nor any co-publisher can accept any legal responsibility whatsoever for consequences that may arise from errors or omissions or any opinions or advice given.

Typeset by Julie Foster
Printed by Clifford Press, UK

# Contents

# Author biographies

**Peter Cossey** is a senior manager in the Capital Markets department of PricewaterhouseCoopers (PwC) in London. Mr Cossey specialises in accounting for derivatives with a specific focus on credit derivatives. He joined PwC in 1988 and spent six years in the audit division, prior to performing a number of consulting assignments in credit derivatives and transaction processing and accounting for leading investment banks.

**Jonathan Davies** is a senior manager in the London office of the International Capital Markets department of PricewaterhouseCoopers (PwC). Mr Davies specialises in the control environments surrounding the credit derivatives functions in banks. He is active in the presentation of conferences, and advises clients on accounting, regulatory and control aspects of credit derivatives. Mr Davies joined PwC in 1994 having worked in the credit function at Nikko Bank (UK) PLC and National Westminster Bank PLC.

**Mark Gheerbrant** is the head of credit trading and structuring at Rabobank International in London. Before joining Rabobank in 1996, he was managing director of the UK Industrial Fund, an institution specialising in mezzanine finance. Prior to assuming this position, he worked for 10 years in investment banking, primarily in derivatives trading and structured finance with Swiss Bank Corporation and the IBJ. Mr Gheerbrant started his career at Arthur Andersen where he qualified as a chartered accountant. He has a degree in Mechanical Engineering from Bristol University.

**Paolo Gribaudi** is a manager at Banca Commerciale Italiana SpA (BCI) in Milan, where he is responsible for credit derivatives activity. Mr Gribaudi has been with BCI for nine years, having joined the company in 1989. He holds a degree in Business Administration from the University of Turin, Italy.

**Michael Haubenstock** is a partner in the Financial Risk Management practice at PricewaterhouseCoopers (PwC) in New York. He has over 20 years' experience in financial institutions. Mr Haubenstock specialises in enterprise-wide risk management and risk capital methodologies for financial institutions. Prior to joining PwC, he worked at GE Capital, AT Kearney Management Consultants and Mobil Oil. Mr Haubenstock holds a BS from the University of Pennsylvania, an MS from Washington University and an MBA from New York University.

**Jane Herring** is the head of credit derivative product management at Barclays Capital Group, which she joined in August 1997. She is responsible for working with the sales force to develop the market for structured credit derivative investments.

Prior to joining Barclays Capital Group, Ms Herring spent three-and-a-half years at CSFP structuring credit- and commodity-linked products.

**Dr Olaf Liedtke** is a financial economist and vice president of Landesbank Hessen-Thüringen in Frankfurt/Main and Erfurt. He studied Economics at the Christian-Albrechts University and the Free University of Berlin, and he holds a PhD in Monetary Policy from the University of Essen. He began his career at the Rhine-Westphalia Institute (RWI) for Economic Research, Essen – one of the six leading research institutes in Germany.

**David Mordecai** is a director of the Commercial Asset Backed Group at Fitch IBCA, where he participates in rating emerging asset-class securitisations. He has previously been an assistant vice president at WestLB, a vice president at an investment bank and a consultant to senior management at a Fortune 100 company. Mr Mordecai has an MBA in Finance from the New York University, Stern Graduate School of Business, and is currently completing a PhD at the University of Chicago Graduate School of Business.

**Andreas Petrie** heads the Capital Markets and Asset Trading Group at Landesbank Hessen-Thüringen, which he joined in 1986. Before assuming his current position in 1994, he worked in the bank's debt origination and loan syndication business, focusing on western European public institutions, banks and corporate borrowers. Prior to this he held the post of regional manager in Asia. Mr Petrie graduated from FH Rheinland-Pfalz with a degree in Economics in 1986.

**Todd Runyan** is a senior manager in the Financial Services Industry Practice of PricewaterhouseCoopers (PwC). Mr Runyan has more than eight years' experience providing accounting and auditing services to domestic and international financial institutions. He has provided assistance to several firms' major banking clients on matters including US GAAP, internal controls, regulatory issues, SEC reporting requirements and accounting issues related to various capital market instruments. Mr Runyan, a Certified Public Accountant, joined PwC in San Francisco in 1992.

**Dr Ingo Schneider** works in the Capital Markets and Asset Trading Group at Landesbank Hessen-Thüringen, where he is responsible for structured products and credit derivatives valuation tools. From mid-1996 to mid-1998, he worked as a swap and interest rate derivatives trader, and before this he was responsible for the market analysis of fixed income derivatives. Dr Schneider gained a PhD in Physics from the University of Frankfurt in 1992.

**Dr Jochen Schober** is chief economist at Landesbank Hessen-Thüringen in Frankfurt/Main and Erfurt. He studied at the Johann Wolfgang Goethe University in Frankfurt and took his PhD in Monetary and Currency Policy. His professional career began at Kreditanstalt für Wiederauf-bau in Frankfurt/Main. Dr Schober is an expert in questions of the economy and of capital market and currency developments.

**Klaus-Peter Schommer** heads the product structuring and risk management team at Landesbank Hessen-Thüringen's Capital Markets Group. He was responsible for establishing the Group in 1995, and has since helped to establish credit derivatives as a new product type there. Prior to joining the Group, Mr Schommer was an interest rate derivatives trader for more than five years. Mr Schommer graduated from the University of Trier with a degree in Finance in 1986.

**Paul Varotsis** heads the credit derivatives team at Chase Manhattan International Limited. In his previous position at Chemical Investment Bank Limited, he helped Chemical's return to the new issues business in the international bond market by structuring and arranging public bond issues and private placements. Mr Varotsis holds an MBA from the Stanford Graduate School of Business, a diploma from Institut d'Etudes Politiques de Paris and a diploma from Institut Superior de Gestion in Paris.

**Hermann Watzinger** is a vice president with Citibank NA in London. He is head of Credit Derivatives Europe with responsibility for developing, structuring and marketing credit derivative products to the bank's European client base. Prior to assuming his current position, Mr Watzinger was a senior transactor in the Emerging Market Derivatives Group. Mr Watzinger joined Citibank in Frankfurt where he was responsible for marketing derivative solutions to the bank's corporate client base in Germany. He holds a diploma from the University of Passau, Germany.

# Credit derivatives: a revolution in the financial markets

Paul Varotsis
Chase Manhattan International Limited

Credit derivatives have formed the subject of many recent talks, conferences and seminars, and some may suspect that they are more about talk than action, particularly in view of the sketchy statistics available. Given that estimated nominal amounts of somewhere between US$150 billion and US$200 billion are barely noticeable when compared with either the derivatives markets or the cash credit markets, it is sometimes difficult to see why so much attention is being paid to these new products and to assess whether they really do represent something new.

However, in my view credit derivatives are changing the financial world, as other classes of derivatives have before them and possibly more so by questioning our banking regulatory framework and breaking down barriers between insurance and banking. They have already helped to modify some crucial aspects of that world, including:

- the structuring of new securities that could not have been available otherwise;
- the pricing of new bond issues, where placement is not driven by cash buyers but by credit derivative aspects;
- the trading of bonds, whether using options to adopt a particular risk profile or shorting credit risk available only in the credit derivatives market for a wide range of names;
- the positioning of spread curves;
- the management of bond and loan portfolios, through the use of leverage and other credit techniques to increase or reduce a risk profile, or increase or reduce the need for funding; and
- the overall management of credit portfolios, where large financial institutions have been actively using credit derivatives to rebalance their portfolios.

It is true that only a relatively small number of financial institutions are actively involved in developing these products. Yet as these applications spread, credit derivatives are likely to play an increasingly important role in the financial markets.

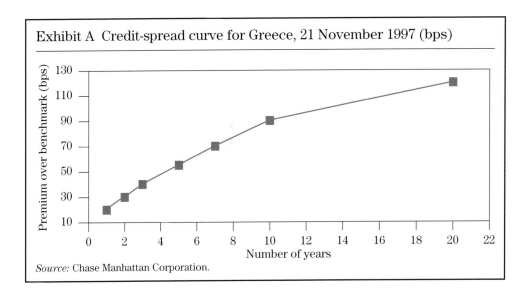

**Exhibit A  Credit-spread curve for Greece, 21 November 1997 (bps)**

*Source:* Chase Manhattan Corporation.

## The distinctive features of credit spreads

In order to arrive at a better understanding of credit derivatives one needs to focus first on credit itself in relation to financial risk management. The basic information about credit risk is concentrated in a credit spread curve, which represents the premium over a benchmark charged to gain exposure to that particular counterparty for a given maturity (see Exhibit A).

It must be stressed that credit is substantially different from other dimensions of risk management, such as interest rates, currencies or even equities.

Firstly, credit risk is extremely diverse. If one compares it with foreign exchange, for example, there are only a handful of major currencies traded in the international markets, compared with thousands of various credits. In addition, for each given issuer one can look at a whole range of different credit risks, from senior secured to preference shares, not to mention the various quirks in documentation. This means that for a single corporate one could develop a whole range of spread curves.

Secondly, although it is now relatively easy to draft a spread curve for a large group of sovereigns, it is still generally the case that the more obscure the issuer, the harder it is to obtain reliable information as to where such risk should trade or might trade. For example, I was recently asked to price such names as Ghana and Uzbekistan, but had little success. However, there is no reason why these could not be priced in due course.

Thirdly, and as a result of this diversity and lack of information, there is little concentration of liquidity in credit spreads, in contrast with what can happen to the common stock of corporates on stock exchanges, or in the T-bill market.

Fourthly, a credit spread for a given instrument reflects at least three dimensions of risk concentrated in one single number: the probability of issuer default; the recovery rate on that particular instrument; and the pattern of offer and supply for the particular instrument. Deriving these three dimensions is still a difficult exercise. Alternatively one can look at the credit world as various sets of options where the holder of a credit position can expect to receive back anything between zero and his principal, depending on whether or not a default has occurred and what the recovery rate could be. This methodology, although quite helpful in valuing credit risk, is still quite different from the way that credit risk is priced in most markets.

Fifthly, credit spreads have often been treated as one-way bets and subjected to changes in fashion, depending on the business environment. In the past few years alone, we have witnessed such movements in the Scandinavian, French, Italian, Japanese and Korean bank markets in succession, not to mention the trends in the various emerging markets.

Finally, although financial theory assumes that the credit spread over the risk-free rate in each country usually refers to that country's own T-bills, credit is not necessarily currency-specific. The spread over a particular country's T-bills may therefore vary depending on the credit quality of the issuing country. In addition, credit is not specific to a given interest rate curve and fluctuations in that curve do not necessarily have an impact on credit spreads. One might wish to position oneself at one point on the interest rate curve of one currency but at a different point on an individual spread curve.

## Credit swaps

Credit swaps are the basic spot instrument in the credit derivatives market and the main building block for a wide range of more complex products.

### Description

The mechanism of credit swaps is relatively simple. For example, a bank may wish to sell risk on a particular corporate to one of its clients. The bank feels that its exposure to that corporate is too high and the client is happy to purchase the risk. The bank pays the client a premium to protect itself against default. If no default occurs, the swap terminates without any additional payment from either party. If there is a default, however, the client that has purchased the risk has to make a payment to the bank.

The premium or spread is the return that the client receives to take the additional risk of the corporate. It could be paid up front or on a periodical basis. Whether it is paid up front or over the life of the contract determines whether and to what extent the client has counterparty exposure on the bank for the life of the contract. It also determines the bank's need for credit lines on the counterparty and for collateral or other types of credit enhancement.

Swaps are therefore terminated at the time of default and marked to market – that is, a payment or delivery is made. These fall into two main categories: cash settlement and physical settlement.

Cash settlement occurs where the buyer of the risk pays the counterparty a sum determined by the level at which a reference asset trades after default. The determination of this sum – the difference between the original price of the asset and its price after default – is usually assessed a few days after the default has occurred, using a dealer panel. Some counterparties have a preference towards an average price determined over a three-month period, as opposed to a single price poll. Average prices are intellectually more attractive, but calculating them involves calling dealers for prices at regular intervals without executing any trades, which makes it hard to obtain reliable prices. The long unwinding period that this approach requires can also make it problematic.

One alternative is to determine in advance the amount due, in what is known as a digital credit swap. These are quite difficult to price and place, and the risk is not easy to manage, with the result that they command a premium which many hedgers consider excessive.

In contrast, physical settlement occurs where the buyer of the risk pays the full value of the principal against delivery of a defaulted asset. The asset being delivered could be either a specific asset agreed in advance, or any financial obligation of the given issuer (which could be loans, bonds or derivative contracts with limitations regarding currency, seniority, structure and maturity).

## Problems of terminology

Currently, 'credit swap' is the term used by most market players, but a number of parties use different labels for the same type of contract. These include 'default options', 'default swaps', 'default puts' and 'credit hedges'.

The direction of a trade must be clearly specified. Using the words 'bid' or 'offer' may be dangerous, as they might express different meanings for the various parties. In substance, the following phrases are synonymous: 'buying risk', 'selling protection' and 'receiving premium'. Thus, for example, if a party says that it is 'buying Russia', one needs to clarify whether it is buying risk or protection. At the moment it appears that the words bid and offer are being more consistently used for buying and selling protection.

The words 'buy' and 'sell' are also widely used in the market, but obviously these transactions are swaps and therefore stay with the parties for the whole of their lives, until they are terminated by a credit event, are unwound or just reach maturity. They are not like cash products, where the responsibility of the party terminates with the sale. The words 'buy' and 'sell' can therefore be questioned, as they normally express a finality that is particular to cash instruments. In substance, we are referring to a hedge rather than an actual sale.

## How credit swaps work

The basic assumption is that by selling a risk to a third party – assuming, crucially, that the default risks of the underlying risk and the third party are not correlated – one can multiply the probabilities of default of the two risks to obtain a combined position that is substantially risk-free. This is generally the arithmetic for risks in the investment grade and good-quality, high-yield categories.

However, if the default risks of the reference asset and the counterparty are correlated the combined position is not risk-free. For example, if one sells Brazilian risk to a Brazilian bank, the combined position is not risk-free, to say the least, as the bank will probably not be able to make the necessary payments if the country declares a moratorium. The relationship between the counterparty and the reference asset is an area of credit derivatives where a great deal of work is still being done, and no single market practice has yet emerged.

## Uses

Credit swaps have developed on the back of structuring, stripping and rearranging credit risk in security transactions. They are convenient instruments that allow the structurer to sell a risk that could not be packaged in the security or, conversely, to originate a risk not available in that format. During the past few years, credit swaps have come to be traded in an interbank market, where various counterparties come to exchange their risk positions. They include:

- credit hedgers wishing to sell the risk as a credit swap, usually to reduce concentration confidentially;
- credit risk investors that see credit swaps as synthetic floating rate notes with such added advantages as flexibility, financial leverage, confidentiality and built-in funding;

- those credit traders wishing to take a particular view on a credit risk, in particular shorting credit risk, that is often difficult to achieve in the cash market; and
- other credit traders wishing to position themselves on one particular section of the credit spread curve.

An example of this last case is a trader who wishes to position himself at the long end of a difficult credit and cover the immediate future. If a default occurs in the near term, the trader is covered, and if the credit turns around, the trader stands to make money as the credit spread tightens.

It should be noted, however, that, being a credit market, the credit swaps market suffers from the same basic drawbacks as other credit markets, particularly the propensity for fashions and one-way bets.

**The state of the market in mid-1998**
Credit swaps are the only credit derivatives that have developed to form an actual market, with hedgers, traders, brokers and end investors. They are the spot side of the credit derivatives market and on a typical day one can find bid/offer spreads for a range of different risks. The more liquid risks are those of sovereigns in emerging markets, in addition to those of whatever credit story happens to be in the news that particular week. If a bank experiences difficulties or is about to be taken over, or if a country is expected to be downgraded or upgraded, its name is likely to appear in the credit swaps market.

Although the market was started by major US banks, such as Bankers Trust, JP Morgan and Chase Manhattan, there is now a wide array of banks active in various market segments. Some specialise in emerging market names, others specialise in corporates; some use credit swaps purely as hedging instruments, others use them only as investments. Insurance companies and a select group of corporates have been active in helping the credit swaps market develop and focus on the aspects that are particular to their lines of business on both the asset and liability sides.

## Total return swaps

Total return swaps are not particular to the credit derivatives market, they are rather generic derivatives adapted to the credit market and its specific aspects.

**Description**
With a total return swap, one leg pays the total return of a given instrument that has a credit dimension, such as a bond, a loan, a convertible, a preference share or a credit index. The other leg, known as the financing leg, bears a synthetic financing cost and is set as a spread, usually over the London interbank offered rate (Libor). The combined instrument creates a synthetic replica of a purchase of the specific underlying asset or index and its associated financing. Total return swaps are thus a lot more specific than credit swaps, which create generic synthetic positions on reference risks.

Total return swaps often involve marking to markets between the counterparties, as well as the posting of collateral. The party selling the total return usually hedges itself by buying the cash instrument. The transaction is quite straightforward, at least from an economic point of view.

**Uses**
Total return swaps are often used as structuring instruments in credit-linked notes

(CLNs), as they allow the structurer to strip the return from its underlying instrument. They can also be used in order to circumvent various regulatory or accounting restrictions. In particular, where a market is closed to certain counterparties, total return swaps offer a convenient means for such institutions to invest in the market synthetically.

Total return swaps are also used as a way of arbitraging funding costs, as a means of taking short positions or as an alternative to repos. Developed below is an example of funding arbitrage.

The higher-level funder buys the total return and sometimes sells the instrument to the lower-level funder, which hedges with the cash instrument. As a result of this funding arbitrage, the buyer of the risk often has to offer credit enhancements (such as rating triggers, covenants or margining) in addition to the regular marking to market, since if one funds at a higher level, one is generally perceived to be of lower credit quality.

The reference asset has to offer sufficient return, after the cost of funds, to justify the whole operation. Therefore total return swaps are very rarely used on high-quality underlying credits and are most often used on high-yielding names.

## Spread options

Spread options originated from a particular market situation. As credit spreads kept tightening, investors complained of low returns, while traders became nervous that their portfolios, which were often worth billions of US dollars, could be subject to large mark-to-market losses if spreads suddenly widened.

### Description

Given this background, spread options were convenient for both sides. Traders were willing to pay a premium that allowed them to reduce their exposure to credit spread volatility, while investors could increase their returns by receiving that premium. The attractiveness of these instruments was enhanced by the fact that traders marked their positions to market while their investor clients did not, as they were held to maturity in their banking books.

### The problem of valuation

Spread options are second-generation derivatives. Credit swaps, like other types of spot instruments, are valued on the basis of market offer and demand, but the valuing of spread options requires the use of sophisticated credit valuation models. Those banks that are active in the spread options market have invested in the infrastructure necessary to value them and manage them in the present market. A general consensus on valuation mechanics is beginning to emerge, but we are still far from any agreement on a single valuation model. The substance of credit risk makes it more difficult to arrive at any agreement, because of the lack of data in a number of crucial fields. Data therefore tends to be either proprietary or too generic to be useful.

### Uses

Most spread options are written between traders and end investors. There does not appear to be anything like a market where positions could be traded among professionals.

# Credit-linked notes

Numerous different types of CLNs have been structured and placed in the past few years. What follows is a generic outline rather than a detailed account of these instruments.

## Description

CLNs are often notes, loans or certificates of deposit with some added credit dimension, usually, but not always, provided by credit derivatives such as those described above. The most basic CLN consists of a bond, issued by a well rated borrower, packaged with a credit swap on a less creditworthy risk. For example, a bank may sell some of its exposure to a particular emerging country by issuing a bond linked to that country's default or convertibility risk. From the bank's point of view, this achieves the purpose of reducing its exposure to that risk, as it will not need to reimburse all or part of the note if a credit event occurs. However, from the point of view of investors, the risk profile is different from that of the bonds issued by the country. If the bank runs into difficulty, their investments will suffer even if the country is still performing well.

## Baskets

In substance the basic CLN just described is what is known as a two-name basket. Investors are often happy to invest in such products, either because the particular risk profile might not be available in another form or because they can obtain additional returns.

Simple baskets of instruments give investors exposure to a portfolio of risks and usually reduce risk through added diversification. A simple basket can comprise a portfolio of well diversified, high-yield or emerging market instruments.

In contrast first-to-default baskets are intended to increase risk and thereby increase returns for investors, which can lose their principal if any of the names in the basket defaults. These more complex credit-linked structures have been available for some years, but they remain difficult to value and their risk is difficult to manage. Nevertheless, they have proved to be attractive to specific investors looking for high returns.

## Leverage

Leverage can be used as traditional financial leverage, in order to increase the return on a given amount of funds invested. The increased return reflects the additional risk taken. Leverage can also be used as duration leverage, where a CLN concentrates the risk of a longer-dated (eg, 10 years) instrument in a shorter-dated (eg, three years) instrument. The principal amount of the note loses or gains value according to the mark to market of the long instrument when the note matures.

## Credit enhancements

By setting a subordinated tranche or subordinating one risk-taker's position to another, an issuer can create various cascading credit qualities within one single type of risk. Alternatively, by agreeing to unwind a trade if a trigger or covenant is hit, an issuer can improve or reduce the credit quality of the various parties in the transactions. Triggers or covenants are particularly useful for taking care of various contingent risks, such as the need to unwind an interest rate swap if the credit quality of the risk worsens dramatically.

## The Chase Secured Loan Note: a case study

Chase Manhattan has developed a structured note, the Chase Secured Loan Note (CSL Note), that covers most of the structuring aspects discussed above. These CSL Notes form a family of products which has proved very adaptable to various types of risk profiles. They therefore provide an appropriate example with which to analyse how credit derivatives can be used in structuring notes (see Exhibit B).

The underlying risk is a portfolio of US loans to corporates rated BB+ to B–. The advantages of this asset class are:

- the loans are senior secured;
- the recovery level in the event of default is usually around 80 per cent, which is high compared with that of similarly rated bonds;
- the loans are made more easily accessible even to those that are not active in the US loans market;
- the prices of the loans generally revolve around par unless there is a major deterioration of credit, in contrast with the high-yield bond market and with emerging markets; and
- there is little interest rate risk, as the loans are based on Libor.

The portfolio is actively managed by a professional fund manager, which is expected to enhance returns of the portfolio. The fund manager is subject to restrictions in relation to concentrations on any single issuer or industry.

Investors obtain exposure to this portfolio through a series of total return swaps. When an investor purchases US$100 million-worth of CSL Notes, the funds are used to purchase high-quality collateral, against which the investor obtains leveraged exposure to the underlying portfolio.

The level of leverage varies between three and eight times, depending on the rating and consequently the position on the risk/return curve where investors wish to place themselves. Various triggers and other tools for credit enhancement are involved in structuring the final product.

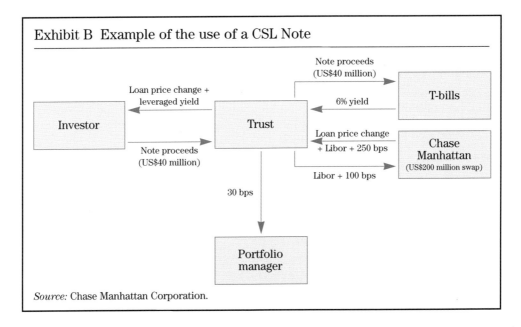

**Exhibit B Example of the use of a CSL Note**

*Source:* Chase Manhattan Corporation.

A rating as high as single A could generally be obtained, offering potential returns in excess of Libor plus 300 for a 10-year note offering periodic puts. A structure which is leveraged six to seven times will receive a BBB rating, with potential returns in excess of Libor plus 10 per cent.

## Conclusion and market outlook

After conquering interest rates, currencies and equities, among others, derivatives are now attacking the largest single aspect of bank and finance management – credit risk – which is also often the defining factor in the traditional banking industry. Credit derivatives have the potential to redefine the way in which credit is managed in the future. However, they still have a few crucial hurdles to overcome. These instruments must concentrate liquidity, overcome legal complexity and regulators' scepticism, and prove efficient under the stress of a credit squeeze. At the same time, the data and models that could transform traditional credit management have yet to be agreed upon.

Chase Manhattan and its competitors are investing resources to respond to these challenges and thus to allow these products to develop in a smooth and useful manner, avoiding any future market shocks as far as possible. There appears to be sufficient momentum and, ultimately, sufficient need from institutions around the world for credit derivatives to be able to overcome such shocks and become basic tools for financial risk management.

# 1

# Credit derivatives in emerging markets: a product analysis

Jane Herring
Barclays Capital

Credit derivatives are over-the-counter derivative contracts the value of which derives, at least in part, from the credit performance of reference assets. In essence, credit derivatives allow investors to trade the risk elements embedded in reference bonds and loans, and to construct synthetically investments with specific duration and credit risk profiles.

This chapter will focus on the application of credit derivatives to emerging debt markets, which offer investors the widest range of debt instruments, risk elements and trading opportunities. The chapter will discuss a variety of credit derivative trades that are now used to meet the investment and hedging needs of emerging market investors. These transactions demonstrate how specific derivative trades can alter the structure of credit risk and how derivative technology can enhance credit portfolio management.

Perhaps the most significant benefit promised by credit derivative technology is the global integration of debt markets. By restructuring the risk/return profiles of credits to meet specific strategies, credit derivatives allow investors to access new markets and asset classes that they could not efficiently reach in the past. In this way, the flexibility of derivatives permits the diversification of debt portfolios.

The recent application of credit derivative technology to bank loans illustrates the potential of derivatives to integrate and energise global credit markets. Commercial banks can now use credit derivatives to repackage and distribute the loans they originate by selling synthetic instruments that create new investment structures based on the unbundled risk components of these loans. In the same way, banks have recently begun to use collateralised credit derivative structures as an alternative to traditional CLOs to efficiently manage credit exposure or reduce their regulatory capital requirements.

Credit derivatives also allow investors to create synthetic loan portfolios without bearing the costs of loan origination and administration. Moreover, they permit investors to take exposure to baskets of bank loans on a credit-enhanced or subordinated basis. In essence, credit derivatives are creating a synthetic secondary market for loans that will fundamentally alter the business of commercial lending.

The products have already made a significant impact on emerging debt markets. These markets present foreign investors with a great variety of credits characterised by higher and more complex risk profiles. Relative to comparable G7 credits, emerging market debt instruments are distinguished by lower credit quality, higher volatility and embedded currency convertibility risk. In addition, emerging market credits are frequently more difficult to access, due to higher transaction costs, unfamiliar operating environments and restrictive tax or regulatory regimes. Credit derivatives can solve many of these problems by offering a set of precision tools that:

- facilitate access;
- optimise exposure; and
- manage risk.

By some estimates, at least half of all credit derivative trades are now linked to emerging market debt. Until very recently, the use of credit derivatives in emerging markets was limited mostly to gaining exposure to hard currency sovereign bonds in global or eurobond form, or to managing the risks associated with holding such instruments. However, portfolio managers are now beginning to apply credit derivatives to local currency instruments, and they can be expected to use them for emerging market corporate bonds and bank loans as well.

## Access

Credit derivatives offer investors exposure to emerging market credits that are otherwise difficult or inefficient to access. By booking derivative transactions and keeping collateral offshore, foreign investors can greatly reduce the regulatory costs and restrictions associated with many emerging market jurisdictions. Funding constrained or leveraged investors such as low-rated banks and hedge funds can also use credit derivatives to access emerging debt markets on an unfunded basis.

## Optimal exposure

Credit derivatives allow fixed income investors to customise synthetic debt securities by cashflow, credit risk and duration. Investors can synthetically shorten the maturity of reference assets in order to create customised exposure for a maturity that is unavailable in the cash market or to take exposure to a particular part of the reference asset's credit curve. For example, investors that want long-term access to emerging market credits but that simultaneously want to hedge short-term default risk can purchase credit-linked notes (CLNs) tailored with a non-default 'lock-out' period.

Investors can use derivatives to create long or short synthetic positions for emerging market bonds and loans. By using credit default swaps, for example, investors can selectively assume default risk on emerging market credits. Or, by using credit spread options, they can monetise investment views on the credit spread movements of reference assets relative to risk-free benchmarks, fixed income indices or other credit-sensitive assets.

## Risk management

Credit derivatives provide a new and much needed set of risk management tools for fixed income investors. Investors can use derivatives to isolate and manage the various risk elements of underlying securities, including:

- specific risk (such as the default and credit spread risks associated with the issuer of the securities);
- interest rate risk;
- regulatory risk; and
- currency and/or convertibility risk.

Using credit derivatives to selectively manage particular risk elements of debt instruments is often far more efficient than selling securities with undesirable risk profiles, especially in emerging markets where wide bid/offer spreads make the liquidation of securities and loans unattractive.

## Structures and mechanics

In emerging markets, credit derivatives involve five basic sets of transactions.

- Financing instruments, such as structured repos and total return swaps, are normally funding-driven transactions that replicate long or short positions in emerging market credits by trading their total returns for fixed or floating rate funding payments. Investors can also use these vehicles to hedge credit risk on portfolio assets or to gain customised exposure to reference credits.
- Credit default swaps isolate the default risk of emerging market credits and transfer it to counterparties in exchange for periodic payments. Investors can use these swaps to tailor the maturity and credit risk of their exposures to specific credits.
- CLNs are structured notes that are linked to the credit performance of underlying assets. Investors can choose principal-protected note structures, which protect a pre-set portion of principal. Or they can use principal-linked structures, which pay enhanced fixed coupons and redeem principal at a rate linked to the credit performance of the reference asset(s). Investors can also use CLNs to create leverage while limiting their risk to the principal invested in the note.
- Credit spread derivatives are options and forwards that are linked to the credit spread movements of debt securities. They allow investors to hedge credit spread risk and to express market views based on the credit spread movements of reference bonds and loans.
- Local currency credit derivatives combine currency forwards and options with credit derivatives. In addition to providing tailored access to local currency debt markets, these transactions permit foreign investors to selectively manage currency and/or convertibility risk, which is usually the dominant risk element in local currency credit markets.

## Product analysis

### Financing instruments
*Structured repos*
Structured repos are flexible repurchase agreements that allow investors to create financing and investment vehicles which are more efficient than those available on the traditional repo market. Investors can use cancellable and convertible repo struc-

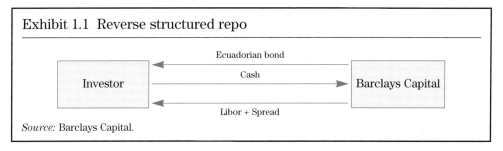

Exhibit 1.1 Reverse structured repo

*Source:* Barclays Capital.

tures to set initial financing at rates well below those available on the plain vanilla repo market. Investors can also achieve superior risk-adjusted returns by using reverse structured repos to hedge credit risk on emerging market bonds.

In Exhibit 1.1 an investor achieves collateralised, above-market, AA-rated returns by using a reverse structured repo to finance a B-rated Ecuadorian sovereign bond for Barclays Capital. The investor pays cash for the bond at the trade date, and at maturity it resells the bond to Barclays at par. In the interim, the investor holds the bond on its balance sheet for one year and earns superior risk-adjusted returns by exchanging the credit risk of the B-rated Ecuadorian bond for the AA-rated counterparty risk of Barclays Capital's parent institution, Barclays PLC.

*Total return swaps*

A total return swap is a derivative contract whereby one party (the rate payer) makes periodic fixed or floating rate payments to another (the total return payer) and receives from the other party the total return – principal and interest payments, plus or minus price changes – of a reference asset for the period of the contract.

Total return swaps can replicate and trade the total performance of most credits, and are especially well suited to the synthetic trading of bank loans. A commercial bank can hedge all credit risk on a loan it has originated, while the counterparty can gain access to the loan on an off-balance-sheet basis, without bearing the costs of originating, buying or administering the loan.

In Exhibit 1.2, an investor seeks exposure to a loan yielding Libor + 275 bps that Barclays PLC has made to a Colombian corporate. The investor enters into a total return swap with Barclays Capital, whereby it pays three-month Libor + 75 bps and receives Libor + 275 bps, plus or minus any change in the market price of the loan. If the loan's market value remains unchanged over the life of the contract, the investor

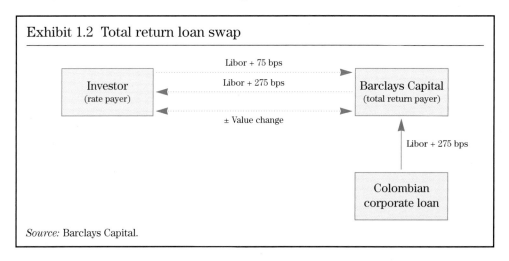

Exhibit 1.2 Total return loan swap

*Source:* Barclays Capital.

earns 200 bps on the transaction. The early repayment risk of the loan transaction would be borne by the investor under the total return swap agreement.

**Credit default swaps**

A credit default swap is a derivative contract whereby one party (the protection seller) receives fixed periodic payments from another (the protection buyer) in return for making a single contingent payment covering losses on a reference asset following a default, bankruptcy or other stipulated 'credit event'. The swap's contingent credit event payment is usually calculated as the fall in price below par of the reference asset, after a pre-determined interval following the credit event. The final price is generally determined by a dealer poll.

Credit default swaps strip off an asset's default risk and trade it separately. The protection seller earns investment income with no funding costs, while the protection buyer hedges the default risk on the reference asset. Credit default swaps allow investors to diversify their portfolios in order to optimise risk-adjusted returns by buying and selling pure credit risk, an asset class with unique investment properties.

In Exhibit 1.3, an investor gains customised, synthetic access to a Mexican corporate bond by selling two-year default protection on the bond to Barclays Capital. The investor receives a fixed premium of 140 bps per annum in semi-annual payments and agrees to make a credit event payment if the borrower defaults on the bond. In the event of a default or other 'credit event', the swap terminates, and the investor pays Barclays the notional multiplied by the percentage difference between par and the bond's final price after the credit event. Alternatively, the investor can settle the swap by buying the bond from Barclays Capital at par.

*Basket default swaps*

Investors can pick up additional yield by selling default protection on several assets rather than just one. In a first-to-default basket default swap, the protection seller assumes the default risk on a basket of emerging market bonds by agreeing to compensate market losses on the first asset in the basket to default.

The UK Financial Services Authority currently requires banks selling protection to adopt an additive approach to the risk weighting of assets in the basket (ie, for assets in the banking book) and to specific risk charges for assets in the trading book (unless the risk is embedded in the form of a CLN that is deemed to be 'qualifying'). Under these guidelines, protection buyers must designate which assets are being pro-

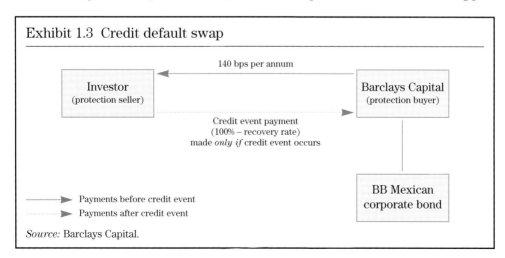

Exhibit 1.3 Credit default swap

140 bps per annum

Investor
(protection seller)

Barclays Capital
(protection buyer)

Credit event payment
(100% – recovery rate)
made *only if* credit event occurs

BB Mexican
corporate bond

Payments before credit event
Payments after credit event

*Source:* Barclays Capital.

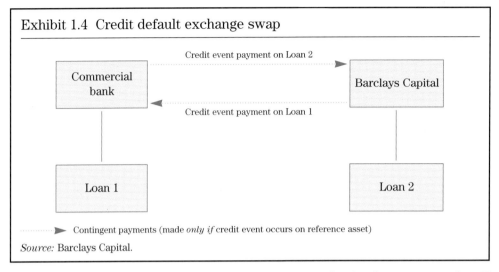

Exhibit 1.4  Credit default exchange swap

Credit event payment on Loan 2

Commercial bank → Barclays Capital

Credit event payment on Loan 1

Loan 1          Loan 2

Contingent payments (made *only if* credit event occurs on reference asset)

*Source:* Barclays Capital.

tected in a basket default swap. For this reason, many banks do not currently sell default protection on a first-to-default or leveraged basis. However, these restrictions do not apply to non-bank investors, such as insurance companies, pension funds and retail investment funds, which prefer cash investments and often sell basket default protection by purchasing basket default notes (see below).

*Credit default exchange swaps*

Investors can also swap the default risk of one asset (or basket of assets) for that of another. In this kind of swap, each party serves simultaneously as a protection buyer and a protection seller. Default exchange swaps are especially suitable for commercial banks wishing to silently hedge the concentration risk on their loan portfolios. Two institutions that lend to different regions or industries can diversify their loan portfolios in a single unfunded transaction, without buying and selling packages of commercial loans.

In Exhibit 1.4, a commercial bank diversifies its portfolio credit risk by trading the default risk of a loan it holds for that of a complementary loan held by Barclays Capital. The investor lays off the default risk on Loan 1, which it owns, in return for assuming the default risk on Loan 2. If one of the reference credits experiences a credit event, then the protection seller for that loan makes a credit event payment to the protection buyer. At this point, the trade could terminate, or it could continue, with the protection buyer in the remaining transaction paying an agreed rate.

If the default risks of the two reference loans are properly matched (as in Exhibit 1.4), both parties will swap contingent payments without making periodic payments. If not, one of the parties will make periodic payments reflecting the difference in default risk between the two reference loans.

## CLNs

Investors can use CLNs to buy or sell credit default protection on reference credits or to create synthetic credit exposure for a maturity not available in the reference credit's outstanding debt issues. These notes are especially appropriate for investors that prefer cash-funded investments, such as insurance companies, pension funds and retail investment funds.

In Exhibit 1.5 an investor uses a sovereign credit default note to sell Barclays Capital default protection on sovereign bonds issued by the Republic of Venezuela.

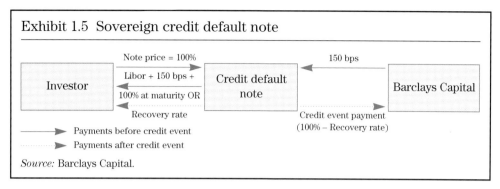

Exhibit 1.5 Sovereign credit default note

Investor

Note price = 100%

Libor + 150 bps +
100% at maturity OR

Recovery rate

Credit default
note

150 bps

Credit event payment
(100% – Recovery rate)

Barclays Capital

——▶ Payments before credit event
········▶ Payments after credit event

*Source:* Barclays Capital.

The investor gains synthetic access to a Venezuelan credit and receives a spread over Libor for a term that is unavailable in the cash market. The investor assumes the full credit risk of the reference bond and may lose all or part of the principal invested under the terms of the CLN.

The investor buys a three-year note at par and receives a coupon of three-month US dollar Libor plus 125 bps. At expiry, the investor redeems the note at par, unless the Republic of Venezuela defaults on any of its outstanding bonds – at which point the transaction terminates and the investor redeems the note for the notional multiplied by the recovery rate of the reference security, which Barclays Capital selects from among all outstanding Venezuelan sovereign bonds.

*CLNs with short-term default protection*

CLNs can also be structured to offer long-term exposure alongside short-term default protection. These notes, which leave investors with forward-starting default risk, are best suited to markets where the risk of default is perceived to be highest in the short term. For example, in markets where a liquidity squeeze and high volatility could produce either default in the short term or stabilisation (and falling spreads) later on, investors can use tailored CLNs to lock in high current spreads (often in a flat yield curve environment) for the long term and protect their principal against short-term default at the same time.

For example, Barclays Capital recently offered investors exposure to 10-year Russian Ministry of Finance US dollar-denominated bonds (MinFins) through a 10-year CLN that pays a high fixed rate coupon and also provides two-year default protection. This note functions as forward-dated CLN, except that the investor receives an attractive coupon (until a credit event occurs) for the first two years, while full principal is protected against default. After this window period expires, the investor continues to receive the same coupon and redeems the note at par after ten years, subject to credit events.

Investors could achieve similar exposure by buying MinFins directly and then purchasing two-year default protection on them. However, because both the cost of short-term default protection and the liquidity premium on these bonds is quite high, the investor would incur a negative net spread for the first two years, in addition to which the protection might not be directly linked to the investor's bonds. On the other hand, the Barclays CLN is structured to pay the same high fixed rate from inception to maturity, such that if Russia defaults on MinFins in the first two years, the investor receives a high fixed rate coupon until default and then redeems the note at par.

*Basket default notes*

Investors can use CLNs to earn additional yield on sovereign bonds by purchasing notes linked to more than one reference obligation. For example, Barclays Capital has issued five-year notes offering exposure to four credits: the Czech Export Bank, the Republic of Croatia, the National Bank of Hungary and the Republic of Poland. The note pays a Deutschmark-denominated coupon of 8 per cent – a rate higher than that of any of the individual reference bonds – and returns full principal at maturity, unless a credit event occurs during the life of the note. The note has a first-to-default structure, such that if a credit event does occur, the investor redeems the note at par multiplied by the recovery rate of the first bond to default.

*Leveraged portfolio notes*

Leveraged portfolio notes are basket default notes that give investors leveraged exposure to a portfolio of reference bonds. This structure allows investors to earn significant returns on higher-grade assets by receiving an enhanced coupon for selling default protection on a number of investment-grade bonds. Although these notes are often applied to high-grade corporate risks, they could equally be used to enhance yield on investment-grade emerging market credits.

Barclays recently issued £50 million of five-year notes linked to the default risk of a £400 million diversified portfolio of UK investment-grade corporate bonds. The portfolio consists of 25 names, each representing £16 million of debt, with an average rating of A2. Investors earn an enhanced annual fixed coupon of 7.50 per cent (or 100 bps over six-month sterling Libor at issuance) in return for bearing the default risk (subject to maximum losses of £50 million) of the entire £400 million portfolio.

If a bond in the reference portfolio experiences a credit event before the note matures, the note's principal is reduced by £16 million times the percentage fall from par of the affected bond. Following the credit event, the note pays the same fixed coupon on the remaining principal in return for bearing the default risk of the remaining credits in the reference portfolio.

The note's leveraged structure allows investors to sell default protection on the £400 diversified bond portfolio, while limiting their potential credit losses to the £50 million principal they have invested in the note. At the same time, the relatively high credit quality of the bonds in the reference portfolio (typically ranging from AA to BBB-) means that the probability of default on any single reference bond is extremely low.

This structure creates a synthetic 'subordinated' note, which is similar to a subordinated CBO, but offers greater transparency – in that the selection of the reference credits is visible to the investor. Investors could earn a similar return by purchasing outright a subordinated bond, for example, but the recovery expectation of such paper would typically be lower than that of senior paper. Moreover, a single subordinated bond would offer no diversification.

Leveraged portfolio notes offer attractive returns to cash investors, such as insurance companies, pension funds and retail investment funds, that seek an enhanced fixed coupon but that wish to avoid exposure to non-investment-grade debt. However, these notes are not suitable for financial institutions, such as commercial banks, that might be forced to risk-weight the exposure to the total notional of the underlying portfolio on an additive basis.

## Credit spread derivatives

Credit spread derivatives are options and forwards linked to a credit spread – the difference between the current yield of a reference asset and that of a benchmark or risk-free security. By separating credit spread risk from market risk and interest rate risk, credit spread derivatives allow investors to fully hedge credit spread risks and to

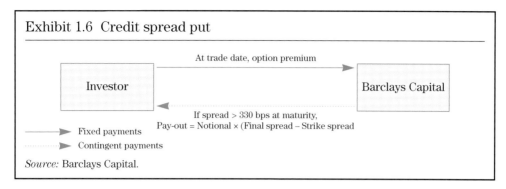

**Exhibit 1.6  Credit spread put**

At trade date, option premium

Investor → Barclays Capital

If spread > 330 bps at maturity,
Pay-out = Notional × (Final spread – Strike spread

→ Fixed payments
····► Contingent payments

*Source:* Barclays Capital.

structure investment strategies based on spread movements. Credit spread derivatives can create long or short exposures to reference assets, with or without leverage.

Whereas default swaps only provide protection against defaults and other clearly defined 'credit events', credit spread derivatives can protect investors from any degree of credit deterioration resulting from such market developments as ratings downgrades, poor earnings or excess assumption of debt.

*Credit spread puts*

Investors can use credit spread puts to hedge against rising credit spreads or to target the future purchase of assets at favourable prices. An investor wishing to buy an asset at a price below market, for example, can sell a credit spread put to target the purchase of that asset, if it expects the credit spread to increase, or simply to earn premium, if it expects the spread to narrow or remain constant.

In Exhibit 1.6, an investor targets for future purchase an Argentinian floating rate sovereign bond currently yielding 300 bps over the benchmark US Treasury. The investor intends to purchase the bond below the current market price in the next year and has targeted a forward purchase price corresponding to a spread of 350 bps. The investor therefore sells for 20 bps a one-year credit spread put struck at 330 bps to Barclays Capital, which currently holds the bond and wishes to protect its market price against any credit spread increase over 330 bps.

If the bond's credit spread remains below 330 bps at the end of the transaction, then the option expires worthless and the investor has earned a premium of the notional multiplied by 20 bps, which it can use to buy the bond at a price below market. If the bond's spread has risen above 330 bps at the expiry of the contract, then Barclays Capital can exercise its option to sell the bond at the strike spread and the investor buys the bond at 350 bps (the strike spread plus the premium), which is the price level it originally targeted. Alternatively, the investor can settle the trade by paying Barclays Capital the notional multiplied by the difference in basis points between the final spread and the strike spread.

The higher the strike spread is above the current spread of the reference asset, the more the credit spread put resembles a credit default swap whereby the investor pays a small fee to buy protection against a massive downward shift in the price of the reference asset. But by setting the strike spread closer to the current spread (as in Exhibit 1.6), investors can use credit spread options to structure precisely calibrated hedging and trading strategies.

*Basket credit spread puts*

As with credit default swaps, credit spread options can also be written on a basket of reference credits rather than just one. In a basket credit spread put trade, for example,

Exhibit 1.7  Credit spread exchange swap

Notional × Spread change between Brazilian Bradys and US Treasuries

Investor

Barclays Capital

Notional × Spread change between Argentine Bradys and US Treasuries

Floating payments

*Source:* Barclays Capital.

the investor increases its premium by selling a number of puts, each linked to a particular security at a particular strike spread. The buyer has the right to exercise the seller into any one of the reference assets at its strike spread, in the full notional amount.

*Credit spread exchange swaps*

Investors can also use credit spread derivatives to speculate on the relative spread between two comparable credit-sensitive securities. The simplest way to do this is by swapping the credit spreads of the reference securities.

Exhibit 1.7 shows a trade designed to monetise the expectation that the credit spreads of Brazilian Brady bonds will narrow relative to those of Argentinian Brady bonds. The investor chooses a spread exchange swap structure that produces a pay-off tied to the difference in the spreads of the two Brady bonds. This structure allows the investor to factor out market risk and interest rate risk to target pure credit spread risk.

The trade uses the exchange of two absolute spreads pegged to a US Treasury to capture the relative spread of two reference securities. The investor pays Barclays Capital the notional amount multiplied by the credit spread between the Brazilian Brady bond and the US Treasury. In exchange, Barclays Capital pays the investor the same notional amount multiplied by the credit spread between the Argentinian Brady bond and the US Treasury.

If the credit spread of the Brazilian bonds falls relative to that of the Argentinian bonds, Barclays Capital will make a net payment to the investor, and vice versa. This kind of trade is ordinarily structured so that no payment is made unless a change in the relative spread occurs.

## Local currency derivatives

Local currency derivatives combine swaps, spread derivatives and notes with currency forwards and options to manage the credit and currency risks of credits denominated in local currency.

In place of simple currency forwards, local currency derivatives usually use non-deliverable forwards (NDFs), forwards settled in dollars – or any other G7 currency – that require no physical delivery of local currencies. NDFs give foreign investors synthetic access to local currency debt instruments without the costs and complications of trading local currencies.

In local currency markets, foreign investors must also manage significant regulatory risk, as well as higher transaction costs resulting from trading, investment and custody taxes and other restrictions that may apply in local currency jurisdictions. Credit and/or convertibility derivatives can allow investors to take a view on local currency markets, while keeping their collateral outside the local currency jurisdiction. Thus investors can greatly reduce their exposure to the regulatory costs and sometimes the punitive taxes associated with these markets. Investors can use credit derivatives to access local currency markets on a cash or leveraged basis.

*Currency-hedged notes*
Investors wishing to take on exposure to local currency bonds without outright currency risk can invest in currency-hedged notes linked to local currency bonds. These notes, which can be written for maturities as short as one year, usually pay a high fixed coupon but bear both credit risk and the risk of the local currency becoming non-convertible.

For example, an investor might purchase from Barclays Capital a one-year currency-hedged note linked to Russian GKO local currency T-bills. The investor pays par for the note and receives a US dollar coupon of 15.2 per cent at maturity, when it also redeems the note at par. However, if a credit or convertibility event occurs prior to maturity, the transaction terminates immediately and the investor redeems the note at par less the credit and currency losses on the underlying GKOs.

*Put options on currency-hedged notes*
Investors can increase their yields on currency-hedged notes by selling the issuer a put option on the underlying bonds. By selling a European put option that allows the issuer to sell the investor the underlying bonds at par at the note's maturity, the investor earns extra spread income for assuming market risk as well as credit risk on the underlying bond. The structure permits foreign investors in volatile local currency debt markets to assume considerable volatility risk in return for substantial spread enhancement.

In the previous example, the investor earns a US dollar coupon of 15.2 per cent for purchasing a currency-hedged note linked to Russian GKOs. But by selling a European put option on the underlying GKOs to Barclays Capital, the investor receives an additional 390 bps of spread (for a total yield of 19.1 per cent) and agrees to buy the underlying GKOs at par if their local market price has fallen below par at the note's maturity. This means that the investor may effectively redeem the note at par less the percentage fall in the price of the reference asset, even if no credit event has occurred.

# 2

# The market participants: applying credit derivatives

Hermann Watzinger
Citibank NA, Global Markets/Credit Derivatives

## Introduction

Credit derivatives: are they just a fashion or are they an important development in the financial industry? Clearly, the answer is that credit derivatives represent an important risk management tool for market participants. They have two major attributes which empower them to grow strongly.

Firstly, they meet enormous demand. Unlike certain market risks, credit risk is inherent in most financial and commercial transactions. All market participants are massively exposed to credit risk and need to be able to manage it.

Secondly, credit derivatives are simple and flexible. In their simplest form, the credit default swap, credit derivatives are very similar to instruments bankers have been using for a long time: guarantees and letters of credit. The difference is that guarantees are static instruments booked in a banking book. They are typically assigned

---

**Exhibit 2.1  Major credit derivatives applications**

|  | Commercial banks | Investment banks | Institutional investors | Insurance companies | Corporates |
|---|---|---|---|---|---|
| Managing credit lines | ++ | ++ | + | ++ | + |
| Optimising returns on economic capital/diversifying | ++ | + | + | ++ | |
| Optimising returns on regulatory capital | ++ | + | | | |
| Managing country lines | ++ | ++ | | + | + |
| Off-balance-sheet financing | + | + | + | + | |
| Exploiting trading views | ++ | ++ | + | | |
| Taking advantage of arbitrage opportunities | + | ++ | + | | |
| Enhancing yields | + | + | ++ | ++ | + |
| Creating tailor-made exposure | + | ++ | ++ | | |
| Accessing new risk | | | ++ | ++ | |
| Managing funding costs | | | | | + |

*Source:* Citibank NA.

to a specific transaction and cease to exist without it. Credit derivatives are booked and managed in a trading book with daily mark-to-market evaluation and are documented under the ISDA Master Agreement. Credit derivatives can transfer credit risk irrespective of an underlying exposure. It is this separation of credit risk from the underlying asset which allows market participants to create tailor-made solutions and to achieve a variety of goals.

While having started exclusively as a banking product, the simplicity and flexibility of credit derivatives increasingly attracts all market participants. This chapter describes the major credit derivative applications for the different user groups (see Exhibit 2.1). The description is to some extent stereotypical as the differences between market participants become blurred with the speed of the market's development.

## Credit derivatives for commercial banks

The competitive situation in the rapidly consolidating banking industry, combined with the pressure from shareholders for an adequate return on equity, is forcing commercial banks to actively manage their credit exposures. Particular attention has been drawn to the capital-intensive lending business.

Credit derivatives are a portfolio management tool that a growing number of banks are starting to use. They allow for the efficient transfer of credit risk without any negative impact on client relationships, because of the confidential nature of the transactions. The dominant instrument is the credit default swap, as the underlying assets are often illiquid banking book assets and the motivation is to manage default risk and not spread widening risk. Transaction size can range from US$10 million for hedging a single name to several billion dollars for hedging a diversified portfolio of names. The main motivations are to create additional borrowing capacity, reduce portfolio concentration and optimise returns on regulatory capital.

### Managing credit lines
Overcapacity in the banking market and disintermediation by investment banks are forcing commercial banks to look for competitive advantages in their corporate banking business.

Buying credit protection on a specific obligor in the form of a credit default swap enables a commercial bank to remain the lender of record under the loan agreement and keep the relationship with the client. At the same time it allows the bank to free up line capacity as the credit default swap transfers credit risk from the borrower to the protection seller. Being able to provide virtually any amount of credit lines, albeit at a cost, and to do this quickly can result in a superior client relationship and more profitable client business.

### Optimising returns on economic capital/diversifying
It is a dilemma for many banks that focusing on their core competencies (ie, lending to certain industries or within a certain region) leads to portfolio concentration. Portfolio concentration means higher losses for a given confidence level and, as a result, the need for more economic capital at the expense of profitability.

Buying credit protection on a specific obligor or on obligors from a specific industry can lower portfolio concentration. The result is a reduction in the amount of economic capital required and a higher return on economic capital.

Better diversification can also be achieved by assuming credit risk. Credit derivatives represent an ideal tool with which to utilise existing credit line availability when there are no client needs due to a lack of relationship with certain target market names.

It has to be said, however, that the active management of economic risk is still very much in its infancy. At the moment, banks are still in the process of identifying their actual exposures and quantifying the resulting portfolio concentration. Many problems have to be overcome in this process, such as the simple incompatibility of loan booking systems or the more complex problem of deriving meaningful volatility and correlation figures from inadequate historical data.

**Optimising returns on regulatory capital**
Many commercial banks have expressed their commitment to corporate relationship banking, which typically includes the lending business. While the return on economic risk might comfortably exceed the lender's hurdle rates, the return on regulatory capital is typically too low for loans to investment-grade corporate borrowers. This is due to the capital adequacy rules laid down by the Bank for International Settlements (BIS), which require a 100 per cent risk-weighting for corporate risk. Credit derivatives allow commercial banks to reduce this high risk-weighting and the resulting capital charge.

A number of US and European bank regulators have issued guidelines on the treatment of regulatory capital for credit derivatives. Although these regulators might ask for different minimum requirements, they will in general allow guarantee treatment for credit default swaps hedging banking book assets. Provided that the swap references the underlying loan and matches its tenor, commercial banks can typically reduce the risk-weighting for a loan (eg, 100 per cent for a drawn corporate loan) to that of the protection provider (eg, 20 per cent for an OECD bank). The regulatory capital which is freed up can then be allocated to higher-yielding businesses or used to buy back equity (see Exhibit 2.2).

This simple example demonstrates how commercial banks can substantially improve the returns of their capital-intensive lending business without impairing client relationships. The assumption is that the capital freed up can be invested in higher-yielding businesses (at 25 per cent pre-tax in Exhibit 2.2).

---

**Exhibit 2.2 Optimising returns on regulatory capital: four-year loan to a corporate borrower at Libor + 20 bps (%)**

|  | No hedge | Credit default swap |
|---|---|---|
| 1. Libor spread of loan | 0.20 | 0.20 |
| 2. Sub-Libor bank funding | 0.15 | 0.15 |
| 3. Cost of default swap | na | −0.25 |
| 4. Net return (1 + 2 + 3) | 0.35 | 0.10 |
| 5. Capital deployed | 8.00 | 1.6 |
| 6. Capital freed up | na | 6.4 |
| 7. Return on capital deployed (invest capital deployed (5) at risk-free rate, eg, Treasury rate of 5.50%) | 0.44 | 0.09 |
| 8. Return on capital freed up (invest (6) at, eg, 25%) | na | 1.60 |
| 9. Total return (4 + 7 + 8) | 0.79 | 1.79 |
| 10. Return on 8% regulatory capital (pre-tax) | 9.88 | 22.38 |

*Source:* Citibank NA.

Aside from the specific advantages discussed above, commercial banks benefit from the quantitative approach that credit derivatives introduce to loan portfolio management. The cost of hedging, for example, puts a market price against the relationship arguments of account managers trying to get a loan approved. In more general terms, Moody's states that in time '... modern credit-risk management and the use of credit derivatives will lead to the reshaping of a new lending culture, one that is increasingly concerned with risk-adjusted earnings and with efficient capital management, rather than as a way to boost assets and market shares'.[1]

Concerning the organisational set-up, it has proved valuable to establish a central risk management group which determines the strategy for credit derivatives activities in the banking book. This unit can bear the cost of hedging as it can demonstrate the institutional benefits of capital management at the top level of management. Together with the credit derivatives structuring and trading department, the risk management group can make sure that the transactions are structured properly and allow for capital or credit line relief. Executing its transactions via the trading unit will enable the risk management group to achieve the best price and structure and to take advantage of the existing operational infrastructure.

### Combining credit derivatives and securitisation

Another popular concept for improving returns on economic and regulatory capital is asset securitisation. For many banks, however, there are two problems associated with asset securitisation. Firstly, it is a funded solution for banks that might not need liquidity due to their high ratings and large deposit bases. Secondly, it requires banks to transfer assets from different branches or different countries into a special purpose vehicle which can cause internal, regulatory, legal and tax problems.

Credit derivatives on single obligors, on the other hand, have only been possible for rated or well known risk, whereas to a large extent loan portfolios consist of unrated and medium-sized companies. In addition, credit derivatives have sometimes been regarded as costly and banking secrecy laws in some countries do not permit the name of a borrower to be revealed.

The solution to these problems is to combine the benefits of credit derivatives and securitisation techniques (see Exhibit 2.3). Rather than transferring a portfolio of loans into a special purpose vehicle, the commercial bank keeps the assets on its balance sheet and buys credit protection on the portfolio in the form of a credit default

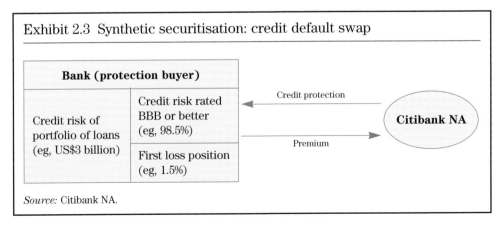

Exhibit 2.3 Synthetic securitisation: credit default swap

| Bank (protection buyer) | | |
|---|---|---|
| Credit risk of portfolio of loans (eg, US$3 billion) | Credit risk rated BBB or better (eg, 98.5%) | |
| | First loss position (eg, 1.5%) | |

Credit protection → 

Premium →

Citibank NA

*Source:* Citibank NA.

[1] S.S. Theodore and M. Madelain: *Modern Credit Risk Management and the Use of Credit Derivatives: European Banks' Brave New World*, Moody's Investors Service, March 1997.

swap. The credit default swap allows the bank to free up regulatory capital and improve its capital adequacy ratios. The way to create a homogeneous asset out of a heterogeneous portfolio of hundreds of loans is to achieve diversification benefits by applying securitisation techniques.

The benefits of synthetic securitisation are as follows:

- It is cheap – the unfunded structure allows banks to preserve their sub-Libor funding spread.
- It is extremely flexible – as assets remain on balance sheet, the structure avoids all internal, regulatory, legal and tax problems which come with asset transfers. Securitisation techniques enable the protection seller to find investors for portfolios of medium-sized and unrated companies, as well as blind pools. Very large size can be accommodated.
- It is simple – confirming the credit default swap is simple, and no issuance of securities is involved.

Requirements for the protection seller are a strong rating, as the structure involves counterparty risk, but also a very good track record in loan trading, asset securitisation and credit derivatives.

### Other applications

*Balance sheet management*
Due to their unfunded nature, credit derivatives are an ideal tool for managing balance sheet size. Total return swaps, for example, allow banks to assume all the economic risks and benefits of a bond, a loan or a portfolio of fixed income instruments while not increasing the size of its balance sheet. It is the total return swap counterparty, the balance sheet provider, which is the legal owner of the asset. For the balance sheet provider, a total return swap represents a short-term yield enhancement opportunity as it receives a spread over Libor for assuming bank risk that is effectively collateralised by the underlying asset.

*Managing country lines*
Unlike investment banks, which use emerging market lines primarily for their capital markets and derivatives activities, commercial banks face emerging market exposure from a variety of sources, such as lending, trade finance or foreign exchange. As a result, freeing up country lines with credit default swaps on specific sovereign bonds results in basis risk. The bank might suffer a loss in its underlying exposure due to a sovereign event, such as inconvertibility of a currency, while the specific bond might not go into default. A way out is to manage country lines with sovereign risk options (for a more detailed discussion see the section 'Credit derivatives for corporates', below).

## Credit derivatives for investment banks

Although the divisions are becoming less distinct, there has been a difference in the approaches to credit derivatives adopted by commercial and investment banks.

While commercial banks concentrate on managing their loan portfolios, investment banks tend to focus on credit derivative applications around bonds. Unlike commercial banks that manage their capital adequacy ratios, investment banks are not restricted to the use of credit default swaps that match the tenor of underlying instruments. Their prime motivation is to manage credit risk in their fixed income portfolios and to create yield enhancement opportunities for institutional investors. This allows investment banks to use the whole range of credit derivative instruments over the whole tenor spectrum.

Due to their typically higher risk appetites, investment banks tend to be more trading-oriented than commercial banks. Investment-grade obligors are less likely to represent underlying risk for investment banks, as traders favour high-yield bonds or emerging market paper due to their higher spreads and volatility.

Typical credit derivatives applications for investment banks include hedging as an overlay strategy, exploiting trading views, creating yield enhancement products and repackaging bonds.

### Hedging portfolios against spread widening

Unlike commercial banks, which are generally unwilling to sell corporate loans for client relationship reasons, investment banks are in most cases free to liquidate their bond inventories if their trading views change. As a result, the ability to hedge the default risk of a specific bond position is of less importance to them.

Investment banks can, however, use credit derivatives as an overlay strategy to hedge against severe widening in the credit spreads of their portfolios. An example of this are three- to five-year out-of-the-money credit spread put options on European government bonds. The option allows for the delivery of, for example, 10-year government bonds at a certain spread over Libor. The motivation is to hedge against a potential spread widening of government bonds during the period of transition to the euro.

### Exploiting trading views

Credit derivatives are an ideal means of exploiting trading views. Buying default protection or credit spread put options is often the only way of going short a specific risk for a certain period of time. Also, it might make sense to go long a specific risk in the form of a credit default swap rather than buy a bond or an asset swap. In many cases credit default swaps offer a better premium than the cash market due to lower liquidity or a different assessment of the underlying risk by the credit derivatives market.

Credit derivatives are an ideal tool for taking advantage of opportunities in the credit spread curve. They allow market participants to break up a fixed income instrument into different tenor brackets and to assume the risk they regard as adequately compensated. While this might mean exploiting a trading view for a bank, it allows institutional investors to create a tailor-made investment to meet their investment criteria (see the section 'Credit derivatives for institutional investors', below).

### Enhancing yields

In the current interest rate environment, investors are looking for yield enhancement products. Embedding credit spread options into asset swap packages allows investors to monetise their spread expectations and enables investment banks to facilitate their fixed income business.

An example of this is a puttable asset swap structure in which the arranging bank improves the return of an asset swap package by buying the right to increase the notional amount at a specified spread within a given period of time.

### Taking advantage of arbitrage opportunities

Credit derivatives techniques can also be an integral part of capital markets-driven transactions. The repackaging of bonds and the creation of synthetic securities represents a fast-growing business segment. By going short certain risks through selling repackaged bonds, banks can take advantage of arbitrage opportunities arising from inefficiencies in the pricing of similar credit risks across different asset classes or currencies.

An example of this is the repackaging of emerging market bonds, which was initially driven by an arbitrage opportunity between relatively high-yielding US dollar-denominated Brady bonds with often irregular cashflows and relatively low-yielding emerging market eurobonds denominated in European currencies such as Deutschmarks.

The arranging bank transfers Brady bonds into a vehicle, rearranges the cashflows and swaps them from a floating US dollar coupon into a fixed Deutschmark coupon with a bullet repayment. Investors are thus able to achieve a higher yield than on a Deutschmark emerging market eurobond with essentially the same risk profile.

The bank arranging the issue is left with a contingent default risk on the underlying Brady bonds. There could be a loss for the bank in the event of a default, as the residual value of the Brady bonds in the vehicle might not be sufficient to cover the bank's potential loss from unwinding the cross currency swap. Credit default swaps with a pay-out linked to the current mark-to-market value of a cross currency swap can be one way to mitigate this risk.

Sophisticated investors who can evaluate joint probability events (in the above example, currency movements and credit risk) can assume this risk and earn returns that far exceed the yields available from purchasing emerging market paper.

## Credit derivatives for institutional investors

It is probably fair to say that the majority of institutional investors have had limited exposure to credit derivatives. This is especially true for fund managers (except managers of hedge funds) and asset managers of insurance companies. If there is exposure, it is usually in the form of repackaged securities. This is as a result of regulatory or internal restrictions on the use of derivative instruments in general. Also, asset managers have typically focused on accumulating a portfolio of high-quality, highly liquid instruments.

In Europe, the introduction of the euro is forcing many of these institutional investors to diversify their portfolios and to change the focus of their activities from currency management to more active credit risk management. On the back of this, we will see increasing use of credit derivatives.

Occasionally, institutional investors use credit derivatives as a hedging tool when the underlying position cannot be liquidated for tax or accounting reasons. The main application for credit derivatives is, however, on the investment side.

### Creating tailor-made exposure

A major problem for institutional investors is the lack of investment opportunities in the cash market that meet their investment criteria regarding risk profile, tenor, currency or type of instrument. Credit derivatives allow investors to create a synthetic, tailor-made exposure and overcome the cash market's limitations.

A synthetic exposure with a tenor shorter than the underlying paper can be created by embedding options into a bond or entering into a contingent forward purchase of a bond. This allows investors to utilise open lines for specific obligors which only have longer-term paper outstanding. The investor assumes the default risk during the period of its investment. The bank structuring the transaction assumes risk on the tail end, ie, it is subject to the risk of credit spread widening until the forward or the option comes into effect. Sophisticated investors are able to achieve very attractive risk/return profiles if they are able to analyse and willing to accept forward credit spread risk.

Another very popular structure among institutional investors has been the repackaged emerging market bond described in the previous section. It allows the emerging market risk profile, the currency and the type of instrument to be tailored to the specific needs of institutional investors in different countries.

Credit derivatives are particularly important for accessing local exposure in emerging markets. Total return swaps can be an effective means for investors of structuring a way around capital market restrictions, such as cumbersome settlement procedures, withholding taxes or minimum holding requirements.

### Accessing new risk

With the introduction of the euro, diversification is the dominant topic in the European investment industry. For many fund and asset managers, the problem with moving down the credit spectrum is the lack of know-how and infrastructure for analysing individual obligors. One way out of this dilemma is to invest in already diversified portfolios of higher-yielding, but still low-risk assets. Commercial and investment banks can offer these diversified portfolios with the help of credit derivatives techniques.

Commercial banks can offer access to credit risk from their high-quality loan portfolios. The argument is that loans and, in many cases, undrawn loan facilities represent an asset class with an outstanding risk-adjusted return due to their low volatility and their higher recovery rates compared with bonds. Credit derivatives, collateralised loan obligations (CLOs) and their combinations allow institutional investors to access this very attractive asset class. The composition of the portfolio can be tailored to the specific needs of the institutional investor. Also, there is no administrative burden of servicing the loans for the investor, as the bank remains the lender of record.

Investment banks provide diversified exposure to European bond markets by offering total return swaps or notes linked to bond indices. A number of banks have recently published bond indices that typically consist of a pool of investment-grade government and corporate bonds with a certain minimum face value. Currently, however, the composition of many indices is still weighted towards sovereign issuers due to the limited liquidity of the European corporate bond market.

### Enhancing yields

Most institutional investors prefer funded assets to unfunded assets and look to charge a premium on credit-linked notes (CLNs) or bonds, as opposed to regular bonds. This is a problem when the underlying risk is investment-grade. The spread charged by the issuer or the effort in using a special purpose vehicle makes a funded solution typically uneconomical, compared to unfunded credit default swaps.

As a result, CLNs providing yield enhancement have been largely limited to emerging market or high-yield exposures and to investment-grade exposures of great size or long tenors.

### Off-balance-sheet financing

Hedge funds are the most active users of credit derivatives among institutional investors. For them, the main attraction lies in the unfunded nature of derivatives.

In total return swaps, hedge funds receive the total return on the assets desired and pay Libor plus a spread. This Libor spread will be determined by the counterparty risk under the total return swap, which will typically only be a fraction of the notional amount. Banks determine the counterparty risk by estimating the maximum likely change in value of the swap contract over the period at risk. They forecast the price volatility of the underlying asset based on historical price changes of the asset and comparable investments.

The bank benefits from the lower joint probability of the swap counterparty defaulting and the underlying asset declining in value. By replacing the credit exposure of a loan with the substantially lower counterparty risk exposure in the total return swap, hedge funds achieve financing at lower spreads.

## Credit derivatives for the insurance/reinsurance industry

There is strong convergence between the insurance industry and the banking industry. The insurance industry is increasingly using the financial markets as a channel through which to distribute insurance risk in order to alleviate capital constraints. Catastrophe-linked bonds are one example of this. The key advantage for financial investors is the lack of correlation with any other financial risks. At the same time, the insurance market can efficiently assume risk from the banking industry. The credit derivatives market mirrors this convergence.

### The insurance industry as a protection buyer

A number of reinsurance companies have used credit derivatives as a hedging tool in order to free up reinsurance capacity for certain types of exposures. For example, many insurance companies are over-exposed to the retail and building sectors.

Due to the peculiarities of the insurance business, the transactions tend to be relatively structured and tailor-made. The main issues to be considered are:

- Basis risk – is it possible to minimise the basis risk between the insurance contract and the credit hedge?
- Trigger event – is there a reference obligation available (eg, a bond or loan) or is it necessary to closely define a specific credit event (eg, bankruptcy, insolvency)?
- Pay-out – will it be a cash settlement or fixed pay-out (eg, 100 per cent)? In some cases a fixed pay-out may be the only feasible solution, because of the need to minimise basis risk or because of the lack of a reference obligation.
- Notional amount – what amount should be hedged, taking into account the cumulative exposure and the recovery value under the insurance contract, both of which are difficult to quantify?
- Cost – are the hedging costs justifiable after taking into account cross-selling opportunities?

Exhibit 2.4 shows a transaction where the underlying risk was a basket of three retail companies domiciled in the same European country:

In this structure the reinsurance company tried to find a balance between a sufficient degree of protection and minimising the hedging cost per name, considering cumulative recovery and risk values, as well as correlation between the retailers. The solution was a basket structure with a digital pay-out. The problem of a lack of reference obligations for the retail companies was solved by defining a specific event under the European country's bankruptcy law which would trigger the pay-out of the notional amount.

A number of factors, such as differing risk assessments or different regulatory requirements, can make these kind of transactions very profitable for both the insurance company and the bank.

---

**Exhibit 2.4  Basket structure transaction**

| *Type of instrument* | *Credit default swap* |
| --- | --- |
| Buyer of protection | Reinsurance company |
| Seller of protection | Citibank NA |
| Tenor | Five years |
| Notional amount | Equivalent of US$20 million |
| Credit event | Liquidation (certain events under the European country's bankruptcy law) |
| Underlying risk | Retailer A, retailer B, retailer C |
| Pay-out | US$20 million for retailer A, US$20 million for retailer B, US$10 million for retailer C, subject to a maximum of US$20 million. |

*Source:* Citibank NA.

---

In addition to buying commercial risk protection, the insurance industry and export credit agencies have started to look into political risk protection using both structured bonds and sovereign risk options.

**The insurance industry as protection seller**

Currently, there is a perfect match between commercial banks and the insurance industry. As described earlier, the rigid BIS risk-weighted solvency requirements are an important motivation for commercial banks' use of credit derivatives. Although the return on economic risk might exceed the internal hurdles, commercial banks are buying credit protection on investment-grade corporate loans in order to free up regulatory capital.

This represents a perfect investment opportunity for insurance companies in the credit risk business. As they are not subject to the same capital rules, they can evaluate credit risk purely from the point of view of economic value. As a result, the premiums that are receivable from these credit default swaps are very attractive. Also, the access to large loan portfolios allows insurance companies to balance and diversify their risk portfolios.

In addition, both commercial banks and reinsurance companies prefer unfunded structures such as credit default swaps. Unfunded structures minimise the cost to the banks and allow the reinsurers to employ leverage.

Although they can be very flexible in structure, most transactions are credit default swaps on large diversified portfolios of loans to identified investment-grade obligors. The insurance company can cover all the losses up to the whole notional amount, or alternatively the risk position can be split into a first loss position (eg, 6 per cent of the notional) and a second loss position (eg, 94 per cent of the notional).

## Credit derivatives for corporates

Over the last couple of years, many corporates have become very sophisticated in their management of market risks, especially foreign exchange and interest rate risks. Most of them are, however, at an early stage when it comes to quantifying and managing credit risk.

At the same time, the credit exposure against important suppliers or clients resulting from long-term contracts or dominant market positions can be very high.

Other substantial credit exposure can arise from project finance undertakings or from counterparty risk to banks. Again, it is important to tailor the credit protection in order to minimise the basis risk between the hedge and the corporate's underlying commercial risk.

Probably the most important application for credit derivatives in the corporate sector is hedging emerging market risk. Here it is important to distinguish between commercial risk (default of a specific company) and sovereign risk (inconvertibility of the local currency or non-transferability of hard currency from the country). While the commercial risk might be acceptable in many cases (for example, on secured loans or intercompany loans), the sovereign risk might require hedging.

Protection from those that traditionally provide protection, such as export credit agencies, private insurance companies or the trade finance market, can be costly or hard to obtain (for example, on intercompany loans). There is an enormous need for the credit derivatives market to become a provider of new protection capacity for generic emerging market activities.

**Sovereign risk derivatives**
It is evident that a typical credit default swap with a trigger event based on specific sovereign bonds does not represent a perfect hedge against sovereign risk. There could be a sovereign risk event without the country going into default on its outstanding hard currency obligations. In this case the protection buyer would not be able to exercise its option, while it would be losing money in its underlying business.

An option on sovereign risk might be a more accurate hedge, whereby if a sovereign risk event occurs, the protection seller has to deliver a pre-agreed notional amount in hard currency to the protection buyer. In return, the protection buyer must deliver to the investor the notional amount in the emerging market currency in the respective country at the then prevailing official exchange rate. (See Exhibit 2.5.)

Consequently, the protection buyer is enabled to transfer money out of the country, although there is an inconvertibility or non-transferability event. On the other side, the investor might be in need of the local currency in any case. Many corporations, for example, are entering into contractual obligations to invest in an emerging market venture at a specified date in the future, in which case they will need to buy local currency. If a corporation has limited flexibility to retreat from its contractual obligations, selling a sovereign risk option would effectively mean selling an option against an underlying position in order to receive a premium.

It has to be said, however, that the market for sovereign risk options is illiquid and availability is limited. The transaction size typically ranges between US$5 million and US$20 million, with tenors of up to 12 months in most cases. For longer tenors, accepting basis risk and hedging sovereign risk with default swaps on emerging market bonds can be a pragmatic way out for corporates.

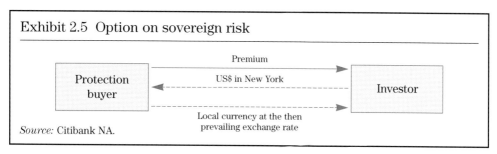

Exhibit 2.5  Option on sovereign risk

*Source:* Citibank NA.

**Other applications**

Although most corporates tend to use credit derivatives as a hedging tool, some have been taking advantage of the yield enhancement opportunities they provide. One popular structure has been balance sheet lending using total return swaps as a substitute for bank deposits.

Another corporate application, although it is in its infancy, is the use of credit derivatives to manage funding costs. Examples of this include locking in credit spreads or monetising expectations on credit spreads in connection with structured funding transactions. There have also been bond issues in which the issuer has provided some credit protection against itself by allowing the investor to redeem early in the event of a downgrade. While the issuer's motivation is to reduce its borrowing cost, the investor has to judge carefully the value of this protection, bearing in mind the identity of the underlying obligor and protection provider.

## Summary and outlook

All market participants need to manage the credit risk inherent in their financial and commercial transactions. Credit derivatives allow them to do so in a relatively simple and flexible way in the form of an overlay strategy.

The volume of credit derivatives transactions in the last two to three years has substantially exceeded market expectations, and the market will continue to grow very fast. There will be some focus on the advanced uses of credit derivatives, but at this early stage of market development the main growth will come from new market players using standard instruments and from increased activity by current users.

Many impediments to market growth are fast disappearing. Documentation is becoming standardised under the leadership of ISDA. More bank regulators are clarifying the treatment of regulatory capital, providing guidelines for many commercial banks and credibility for the market. More commercial and investment banks are starting up credit derivative departments as a response to internal needs and in search of new revenue opportunities. After having researched market risk management models in depth, the banking industry is now focusing on a quantitative approach to credit risk management, which in time will lead to a surge in credit derivatives activity for the management of economic capital. The decline in spreads and the introduction of the euro will sharpen the credit awareness of Europe's institutional investors, and on the back of this we will, again, see more credit derivatives activity. Finally, the convergence of the insurance and banking industries continues to gather pace, and this too is promoting increased use of credit derivatives.

Finally, the combination of credit derivatives and securitisation techniques has opened up a new dimension for the credit derivatives market. This will allow the market to expand into new asset classes, such as mortgages, credit cards and consumer loans. In the not so distant future credit derivatives will no longer be seen as an art form; they will instead simply become the unfunded means of transferring risk.

# 3

# Risk management in a credit derivatives business

Michael Haubenstock, Peter Cossey and Jonathan Davies
PricewaterhouseCoopers

Credit derivatives permit the trading of credit risk without actual ownership of the loan. They provide a relatively efficient and flexible mechanism for selling, acquiring or arbitraging credit risk and for managing regulatory capital. As credit derivatives do not require interaction with the original borrower, they enable users to diversify risk and access new clients and investments, while leaving original customer relationships undisturbed. Since many institutions are reluctant to sell underlying assets for fear of upsetting business relationships, credit derivatives may become one of the most important portfolio management tools of the next century.

Recent estimates of the market's potential size in the year 2000 range from US$100 billion to US$1 trillion, more than triple the estimates of the current market size. With fast-growing volumes and a relatively young and dynamic market, financial risk managers face a multitude of challenges in managing and controlling the risks involved. The nature of new credit-related instruments – be they credit derivatives products, structured notes or similar instruments – may require that both market and credit risk management groups change the ground rules and methodologies commonly used for evaluating and controlling risk in many products today.

Credit derivatives are different from traditional derivative instruments. Firstly, they include two sources of credit risk: that of the protection buyer or protection seller, and that of the underlying asset that is being bought or sold and is impacted by the soundness of the borrowing entity (called the 'reference credit'). For most traditional instruments, the primary risk is interest rate, exchange rate, commodity or equity risk. In addition, there is the credit risk of the counterparty. The unique feature of credit derivatives is that the primary underlying risk is the credit risk of the counterparty or the reference credit. This requires the adaptation of systems, methodologies and the risk management approach.

Another differentiating factor in credit derivatives is that although they can be considered a trading instrument, the key risk driver is credit risk rather than market risk. Modelling credit risk today at the transaction or the portfolio level is especially challenging since there are no universally accepted credit risk models and little good historic data. The industry is, however, moving towards universally accepted standards with several public domain products (eg, CreditMetrics, KMV and CreditRisk+) vying for attention. Nevertheless, currently it is difficult to aggregate exposure from credit derivatives into appropriate credit limits and portfolio measures.

The existing regulatory environment for credit derivatives is at times unclear and often inequitable. While some regulators have issued guidelines regarding the relationship between credit derivatives and banking books, the guidelines are not wholly in line with other standards enacted for trading books, nor are they internally consistent. The primary motivation for using credit derivatives is often the reduction of regulatory capital to support general banking risk. At times, however, the regulatory environment can actually create regulatory capital penalties for using credit derivatives. The purpose of this chapter is to explore the risk management issues for those banks that use or trade in credit derivatives.

## Types of credit derivatives

The total return swap and the credit default product are the most common types of credit derivatives in the market today. The main difference between them is that a credit default product transfers purely credit risk, while a total return swap transfers

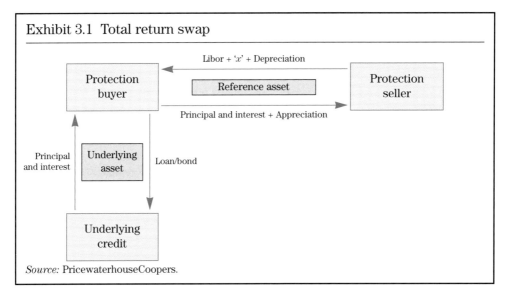

Exhibit 3.1 Total return swap

*Source:* PricewaterhouseCoopers.

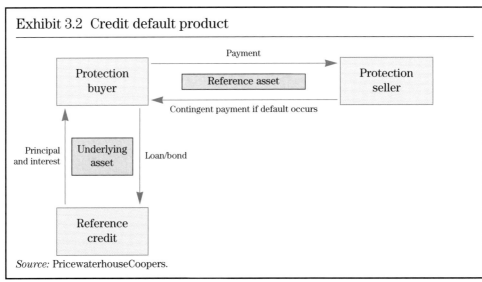

Exhibit 3.2 Credit default product

*Source:* PricewaterhouseCoopers.

both credit and market risk. In a basic total return swap, the protection buyer – for example, a commercial bank seeking to liberate capital or to reduce credit exposure to a certain customer – enters into a total return swap with a protection seller, which is often another bank or investor (see Exhibit 3.1).

The legal documentation between the buyer and the seller specifies a 'reference asset'. This is a particular loan or bond that is used to determine the price and the conditions of default for the credit derivative transaction. The protection buyer makes payments to the protection seller of all cashflows arising from the reference asset, plus positive mark-to-market movements of the reference asset. The protection seller pays to the protection buyer Libor + 'x' bps, plus any negative mark-to-market movements in the reference asset. In this case, both the credit and market risk of the reference asset have been transferred. The reference asset may or may not be the same as the underlying asset that the protection buyer is trying to hedge.

A basic credit default product differs from a total return product in that the protection buyer transfers to the protection seller only the default risk of the reference asset (see Exhibit 3.2).

The protection buyer makes fixed payments (generally in advance) to the protection seller. The protection seller makes a contingent payment to the protection buyer only when there is a 'credit event', which is specifically defined in the documentation. Typical credit events are failure to pay or a downgrade. If no credit event occurs, the contract expires without any additional payments.

## Sources of risk

To understand the risks involved in credit derivatives, one must analyse a multitude of risks that stem from various sources. These risks may be broadly grouped into four general classes: credit risk, liquidity risk, market risk and operational risk. This section describes the many component parts of each of these four general classes of risk.

### Credit risk

Not surprisingly, credit risk is the primary risk driver associated with credit derivatives. Several types of credit risk are inherent in these products, including counterparty risk, reference asset default risk, specific risk, correlation risk and basis risk. The applicability of each of these risks depends on whether one is the protection buyer or seller. Exhibit 3.3 identifies which risks apply to each type of product and how they differ for protection buyers and sellers.

#### Counterparty risk

Like most other derivative products, credit derivatives generally involve counterparty credit risk.[1] The counterparty is the primary party on the opposite side of the trade, often another banking institution or a corporate entity. Counterparty risk is the risk that a counterparty to a financial transaction will fail to perform according to the terms and conditions of the contract. The term counterparty risk is usually used for instruments with a mark-to-market value. It is measured as the positive mark-to-market value that represents the replacement cost in the event that the counterparty defaults.

Both the protection buyer and the protection seller can incur counterparty risk. In the case of a credit default swap in which the fixed payment is made in advance,

---

[1] Two credit derivatives that do not carry counterparty risk include credit-linked notes (to the issuer, not to the borrower – because cash is received) and collateralised transactions.

**Exhibit 3.3  Levels of risk on credit derivative products**

| | Protection buyer | | | | | Protection seller | | | | |
|---|---|---|---|---|---|---|---|---|---|---|
| | Counterparty risk | Reference asset default risk (if owned) | Specific risk | Correlation risk* | Basis risk | Counterparty risk | Reference asset default risk (if owned) | Specific risk | Correlation risk* | Basis risk |
| Total return swap | XX | None | | XX | XX | XX | XX | X | | |
| Credit default product | XX | None | | XX | XX | X | XX | X | | |
| Basket swap | XX | None | X | XX | XX | X | XX | | XX | |
| Credit-linked note | None | None | None | None | XX | XX | XX | X | | |

\* Joint probability of default (counterparty and reference credit).

*Source:* PricewaterhouseCoopers.

the counterparty risk is borne wholly by the protection buyer. In the case of a total return swap, both the protection seller and the protection buyer bear counterparty risk, since both sides make payments during the life of the transaction, and thus, each sees the other as a counterparty.

*Reference asset default risk*

One of the unique characteristics of credit derivatives is that they include a second source of credit risk – the reference asset. A protection buyer typically has credit exposure to a single customer or group of customers that it is trying to hedge. Such customers are called the reference credit. The documentation, however, will include a reference asset, which may or may not be the same as the underlying reference credit. There are a number of reasons why these may differ.[2] One of the primary reasons why the documentation includes a reference asset is that the protection buyer may not necessarily have a position it wants to hedge; it may just wish to short a credit. A further reason for the existence of a reference asset is the need for an instrument that has liquidity and observable market prices.

The protection seller is providing credit protection for this reference asset, and consequently assumes the credit risk if a defined credit event of this asset occurs. It does assume the risk of default on the reference credit (sometimes referred to as the underlying asset) – unless, of course, the reference asset and reference credit are identical. This distinction is often confusing. Payment is triggered by any of the credit events specified in the documentation – for example, failure to pay, cross default, cross acceleration, material restructuring and/or repudiation.

Protection sellers are in fact acquiring credit exposures, just as they would in loan or bond issuances, but they are often acquiring these exposures without funding them. This can be a useful strategy for banks running high funding costs. Such banks are, in effect, exposed to credit events of the reference asset. In default swaps, they are exposed only to a default event. In a total return swap, they are exposed to all

---

[2] This mismatch results in a further risk – basis risk – as described later in this section.

credit events and market price movements during the life of the total return swap (see the section 'Specific risk', below). For other types of credit derivatives, the exposure to credit events depends on the details of the transaction.

As for protection buyers, they are effectively replacing their reference credit default risk with counterparty risk (assuming that the reference asset equates exactly with the reference credit). For the protection buyer to experience a loss under a default swap, both the reference credit and the protection seller must default. The protection buyer counts on this lower probability of a joint default. If the probability of a joint default is not minimal, the pricing of the instrument should reflect this fact. The probability of joint default is clearly an important factor in determining the effectiveness of an intended hedge.

### Specific risk

Specific risk is the impact of credit risk on market risk; however, it is usually classified and managed as credit risk. Some credit derivatives are subject to changes in the market's perception of the reference credit's creditworthiness. A downgrade in the reference credit's credit rating will typically result in a higher spread and a lower price, and, in certain transactions, may trigger a credit event. In a total return swap, the total economic performance of the reference asset is transferred to the protection seller. Therefore, any change in the reference credit's credit rating may result in a change in the value of the reference asset, and consequently, the credit derivative. Any negative news or other market perception can have a similar effect.

### Correlation risk

Participants in the credit derivatives market are exposed to several types of correlation risk. First of all, the protection buyer is exposed to correlation risk between the counterparty and the reference asset. In order to produce an effective hedge, it is important to ensure that the joint probability of default by both entities is low. Alternatively, if the probability is not low, the pricing should reflect the increased risk.

For instance, a protection buyer may want to think twice before embarking upon a credit derivative transaction with a Korean bank to hedge an exposure to another Korean company. Such a protection buyer may want to consider a counterparty with a different geographical base. Alternatively, the protection buyer could enter into another trade to attempt to hedge its Korean banking sector risk. The key point is that the protection buyer should clearly identify exactly what risk it is attempting to hedge, for example:

- specific corporate risk (ABC Ltd in Korea);
- industry risk (banking);
- geographical risk (Korea or other emerging market); or
- a combination (Korean banking).

If an institution wishes to hedge a Korean bank and believes that emerging market countries (such as Russia) are highly correlated with Asia, then buying protection on the Korean bank from a Russian bank counterparty would not be an effective hedge.

The second type of correlation risk applies primarily to credit derivative products that involve multiple reference assets (such as basket swaps). The correlation risk refers to the probability that a credit event (downgrade or default) for one of the reference assets in the derivative will affect the value of the other assets referenced in the contract.

From the perspective of the protection seller, understanding the impact of correlations on the overall risk of the credit derivative is imperative for the adequate pricing of the risk.

*Basis risk*

Basis risk is incurred by the protection buyer when the reference asset used for the transaction does not exactly match the characteristics of the underlying asset or reference credit that the protection buyer is trying to hedge. To improve liquidity and to assure the availability of price quotes, users of credit derivatives often select as the reference asset the most widely traded bond of a borrower, regardless of the underlying asset being hedged. The reference asset is often a senior unsecured bond, although the protection buyer may be hedging a loan. Bonds and loans have different seniority, liquidity, spreads, recovery rates and tenors; therefore, in the event of default, the credit derivative may not recover all of the loss, as it was intended to do. This mismatch is the major source of basis risk in credit derivative transactions.

Protection buyers also face basis risk when there is a mismatch between the trigger event on a reference asset and an actual event that causes loss. For example, a bond may have its rating downgraded for perceived or actual credit reasons, but the 'credit events' specified within the documentation may not have included a ratings downgrade. Accordingly, the spread would have widened and a loss (albeit unrealised at this stage) would have been incurred; however, no default pay-out would have been triggered to mitigate this loss.

A further risk is assumed when the detailed credit events included in the documentation do not exactly match the legal terms of the underlying asset (for example, a loan or a bond). This risk is exacerbated with loan exposures because they often contain non-standard terms and conditions, and it may thus be difficult to obtain an exact match with the credit events specified in the derivative. This mismatch exposes the protection buyer to a default on the underlying asset that does not trigger a pay-out under the credit derivative contract. Such a risk is sometimes called 'documentary asymmetry'.

**Liquidity risk**

Liquidity risk arises when a position in a particular instrument cannot be either bought or sold without moving its price, or when the bid/ask spread is so wide as to make it difficult or uneconomical to liquidate or hedge. In credit derivative transactions, liquidity risk arises in three ways. Firstly, credit derivatives still trade in a very young market. Trading volumes are relatively low and products are not standardised. Therefore buyers and sellers are sometimes unable to find counterparties for their transactions. Nevertheless, liquidity will most likely improve within a few years, given the market's current dramatic growth.

A second source of liquidity risk stems from the reference asset. Ideally, credit derivatives should be referenced to an asset that is widely traded and for which the prices are readily available. At settlement, if the reference asset is illiquid, the value of the credit derivative can be distorted. Of course, if a trade needs to be settled due to a default, this is exactly the time when liquidity will dry up – which magnifies the problem.

The third source of liquidity risk relates to the structuring or selection of appropriate credit derivatives. For instance, if there is a mismatch between the maturity of the credit derivative and the maturity of the underlying asset for which a hedge is attempted, the protection buyer will either lose its hedge or need to replace the credit derivative transaction. When the transaction matures, there could be poor liquidity, or else the market pricing might have changed, making it uneconomical to replace the contract. This particular type of liquidity risk is called 'roll-over risk'.

## Market risk

Credit derivatives contain two sources of market risk: interest rate risk and credit spread volatility. Movements in interest rates affect the discounted value of expected cashflows; consequently, they affect mark-to-market values.

Credit spread volatility refers to changes in market spreads (over the risk-free rate) within a given rating category. This risk is considered a market risk, while changes in spreads due to credit events, such as ratings migrations, are considered credit risks (see the section 'Specific risk', above). Credit spreads are affected by macroeconomic factors, such as overall demand in the bond market, and by industry trends and exposures. They are proven to change over time and need to be reflected in risk assessment and measurement.

## Operational risk

'Operational risk' is a catch-all term that includes those risks that are not traditionally quantifiable in the way that market risk and credit risk are quantifiable. Included under the general category of operational risk are a wide variety of surprises at the cost of doing business: control risks, legal risks and technology risks, to name but a few.

The operational risks that are specific to credit derivatives include suitability risk; legal and regulatory risk; documentation and settlement risk; model risk; systems risk; organisational risk; and reputational risk.

### Suitability risk

Suitability risk (or moral hazard risk) is the risk that investors or counterparties are not fully aware of the inherent risks of an instrument. There is a risk that they may use instruments that either are not appropriate to the risk profile of the institution or that depart radically from what has been approved by management.

Given the infancy of the market and the rapid development of sophisticated products, many investors will not be acquainted with the dangers inherent in the use of credit derivatives. Therefore institutions should be well aware of suitability issues. Suitability risks are particularly sensitive. If they are not managed properly, the reputation of the organisation may be put at risk.

### Legal and regulatory risk

While regulators are continually updating guidelines, they cannot keep ahead of the new products that are being developed. It is crucial that participants in the credit derivatives market keep abreast of the guidelines under which they must operate.

Considerable ambiguity still surrounds the supervision of credit derivatives. In the United States, the Federal Reserve Board and Office of the Controller of the Currency have issued preliminary guidelines regarding the use and treatment of credit derivatives. In Europe, guidelines have already been issued by regulators in the United Kingdom and France, and are imminent in Germany.

As new and innovative products continue to be developed, participants in the credit derivatives market run the risk of having to follow regulations that negate or run counter to the original intent of the product. While the intent of a credit derivative may be to decrease the capital requirements of an institution, regulations may result in a capital penalty for using the credit derivative. As a result, the required capital may actually increase.

When credit derivatives were first introduced, US regulations stipulated that capital must be calculated in accordance with approach adopted by the derivatives themselves. In the case of a total return swap, the protection buyer had to hold the underlying asset at a 100 per cent risk weighting and the swap at 20 per cent. Meanwhile, the protection seller only had to hold the swap at 20 per cent. As a result, the counterparty with the lower risk had the higher capital requirement. The guidelines have since been updated to reflect a more equitable distribution of capital. The 'direct credit substitutes approach' requires the protection buyer to hold the regulatory guaranteed asset at a 20 per cent risk weighting, while the protection seller treats its exposure as a standby letter of credit with a 100 per cent risk weighting.

European regulators are currently discussing at length whether credit derivatives are options, swaps or indeed some new family of default products. This definition is important, for example, in Germany, where the definition of a contract as a swap or an option may affect its regulatory treatment.

In some countries, certain credit default products may be regarded as insurance against non-payment or insolvency of the reference credit. (This type of classification varies with the particular terms of the contract and the country in which the credit derivative is structured.) US and UK regulators do not consider credit derivatives to be insurance products, due to their fungible nature and due to the fact that under insurance contracts one must incur loss and one cannot profit from an actual loss. With a credit derivative, protection can be taken and a pay-out received when no actual loss has been incurred. (For example, if a credit was shorted or basis risk worked in the institution's favour.) Furthermore, in a leveraged deal, a bank could find that the protection exceeds any actual loss on the underlying asset.

Nevertheless, banks doing business in other countries should examine whether entering into a particular credit default contract could constitute insurance business under any of the relevant jurisdictions and whether the bank would require authorisation from an insurance regulator. More importantly, perhaps, if a counterparty in a different jurisdiction is deemed to be carrying on insurance business, there is a chance that the contract may become null and void. This could render the protection that was purchased ineffective.

Credit derivatives have also often been likened to guarantees. While certain credit derivative products do in fact have characteristics that are similar to guarantees, they are not deemed to be guarantees due to the strict legal definition of a guarantee. A guarantee is geared much more towards protecting a party from an actual loss and ensuring that the party is compensated for such a loss. The nature of credit derivatives is that not just non-payment, but any number of credit events, may constitute default. Credit derivatives then require a calculation to estimate loss. This is often a difficult calculation to make if the reference asset is an instrument that is not publicly traded.

Finally, banks need to ensure that the credit derivative transaction is not deemed to be 'gaming'. Such a classification might result in the contract's transgressing the regulations of the relevant jurisdiction and might possibly even jeopardise its validity. Although gaming is not considered an issue in the United States or the United Kingdom, it can pose problems in certain other countries. A recent deal in Russia is rumoured to have come up against the implications of gaming. This issue is particularly important because of the proliferation of cross-border transactions for credit derivative products.

*Documentation and settlement risk*
The International Swaps and Derivatives Association (ISDA) has developed some

standardised documentation for master agreements and plain vanilla credit derivatives. However, there is still plenty of room for interpretation. Documentation risk stems from the contract specifics regarding what determines a trigger event, who monitors the transaction and what consequences result from the trigger event.

For instance, if a loan is used as the reference asset, the protection buyer may not be able to claim a default unless the default is publicly available information (PAI). PAI is typically defined as occurring when two or more news disseminators carry information about a credit event. Situations have arisen whereby an event has been triggered, but the protection buyer cannot enforce it due to confidentiality (ie, there is no PAI). When the event of default, such as non-payment, is not clear, well defined legal terms are needed to avoid potential future disputes.

Due to the early stage of the market's development, no credit derivative contracts have yet been tested in a court of law. There have been a number of defaults, however, particularly in Asia, where the two counterparties and their calculation agents have had to negotiate a suitable compromise. The protection offered by these contracts has yet to withstand rigorous litigation.[3]

Intricately entwined with documentation risk is settlement risk, which involves the ambiguity surrounding what will be delivered upon settlement, when it will be delivered and how it will be delivered. For example, in cases in which the protection buyer does not own the reference asset, there is a risk that the reference asset may not be available for physical delivery upon settlement – or indeed that the asset may itself be non-transferable. To mitigate this risk, a protection seller may want to include in the documentation a provision for settlement by the physical asset or by cash value. The protection seller should ensure that there are no legal or other reasons why it should not hold the underlying asset if it is delivered. This has proved particularly relevant in Japan, where certain Japanese institutions selling protection have found that they are not allowed to hold the bonds deliverable under the contracts.

*Model risk*

The development of credit derivatives has hastened the need for accurate internal valuation models.[4] Quantitative models are necessary for many purposes, including pricing credit derivatives; evaluating institutions' hedging and capital requirements; calculating the credit risk of existing portfolios; performing marginal analysis for credit exposures; and measuring market risks.

While various models are available in the market, they are only as good as the assumptions and data that they contain. If the quality of the data that is used in a model is inadequate, the results may be misleading. Bond default data on public companies is plentiful in the United States, but information on certain companies and on other credit instruments is still relatively scarce and of low quality.

Models and their inputs need to be continuously stress-tested for quality, sensitivity and completeness of coverage. Models also need to be back-tested against the market and their outputs examined with a very critical eye. It is worth noting, however, that in contrast with the short-term horizon that is typical of value at risk (VaR) calculations, credit risk models normally estimate the probability distribution of cred-

---

[3] There has been a recent court case in Asia rumoured in the press to be based on credit derivatives. The key issue was the plaintiff's plea of not being informed of the risks, rather than the court's having to test default criteria.

[4] In fact, regulators are currently examining the approach of internal models to measuring credit and market risks for credit derivatives.

it loss over a long time horizon – ie, a year or more. It is extremely difficult to accurately back-test a model's fitness to estimate the unexpected credit loss that could occur over the course of a year.

*Systems/IT risk*

Given the fact that credit derivatives are so new, many systems cannot accommodate them. Thus participants in the credit derivatives market face the considerable risk of having incompatible systems and system work-arounds. Given the broad range of risks inherent in the credit derivatives market and the continual development of new products, systems need to be flexible and comprehensive. They must be able to handle a wide variety of asset types and configured for use by many different groups within the organisation. They also need to be able to accommodate other risks.

*Organisational risk*

Credit derivatives business involves many organisational entities, including the trading function (the market-makers), who buy and sell the instruments; portfolio management or other users, who enter into credit derivative contracts to hedge or acquire credit exposures in loan or investment portfolios; and the various risk management and approval bodies. As credit derivatives are still relatively new instruments, certain organisational roles and responsibilities may not be fully defined. There may be conflicts between groups as to who should be responsible for each function and who should have authority over whom. There may also be responsibilities that fall into the cracks between the various groups.

One example of the risks resulting from organisational issues involves independent price verification. It may be that traders do not allow their middle office to obtain price quotes from outside their organisation, because of the lack of transparency in the credit derivatives market. This situation results in a conflict of interest, because the middle office cannot then obtain independent price verification for credit derivatives. Instead, it has to rely primarily on challenging the traders' assumptions in the model, thereby creating greater friction and increasing the risk that incorrect or inaccurate pricing will remain undetected.

There is also a risk that some of the relevant entities – particularly the middle or back office, internal audit and risk management areas – may not fully understand certain credit derivative transactions. This could be the result of poor communication with the traders, confusing front-office jargon, or new and exotic structures. As a result, there may be considerable risk to the organisation in terms of documentation, reporting and monitoring.

*Reputational risk*

Investment banks have to be aware of reputational issues. A situation could easily occur whereby an institution has a loan that is about to default, and has also gone short in the trading function to hedge this position. The bank needs to address carefully whether this is unauthorised use of client confidential information, or even insider trading. To combat this issue, the bank will need to ensure that there are adequate Chinese walls in place.

## The risk management process

We have outlined many of the types of risk that financial institutions face when they buy and sell credit derivative products. As with any other financial product, the risk management process mandates that all the relevant risks must be systematically identified, measured and managed.

The best way to support the risk management process is with an infrastructure of people, processes and technologies. Such an infrastructure should include an organisation; an approval process; a risk measurement process and risk limits; and policies. This section describes some of the major elements of a risk management process for credit derivatives.

## Organisation and people

Two internal groups are typically involved with credit derivatives: the portfolio management function and the trading function of the lending organisation. The portfolio management function uses credit derivatives to hedge concentrations in individual names or market segments. Portfolio management may also be an investor (ie, it acquires risks), or it may be motivated by the need to reduce regulatory capital. The trading function creates products for customers and may also engage in proprietary trading. Normally, the portfolio management function operates on an accrual basis for accounting purposes (although it could be managed on a mark-to-market basis), while the trading function operates on a mark-to-market basis. Obviously, the risk measurement and management processes for these two types of activities will differ significantly.

All credit derivatives activity is supported by independent risk management functions. Major institutions typically have three relevant functions: credit risk management, market risk management and product control.

- *Credit risk management:* this function establishes credit risk policy; sets counterparty and reference credit limits for credit derivatives; develops migration analyses and default probabilities to use in pricing; sets provisioning policies; and rates counterparties. Credit risk management may be divided between the trading area and the lending side, with separate approvals needed from each.
- *Market risk management:* this function sets market risk policy; establishes limits for market risk; and develops measurement methodologies, such as VaR.
- *Product control:* this function performs revaluations; analyses profits and losses; sets reserves; monitors capital usage; and issues financial reports.

Given the multi-dimensional aspect of credit derivatives, the various risk management functions must work together very closely in order to understand the overall risks involved. Risk policy may require approval by one or more of these groups for individual transactions, as well as for counterparty credit lines.

Several other support and control functions may also be involved in the risk management process for credit derivatives. For instance, a legal function would most likely be involved in contracts and documentation control; the asset/liability (Alco) function may be charged with the supervision of market risk exposures; and the IT function needs to be involved in systems compatibility issues.

## Analysis and approval

Given that credit derivatives have characteristics that resemble traditional financial products (such as loans and guarantees) and derivative products, they require some of the same types of credit risk procedures. Determining the credit quality of a counterparty or reference asset involves the same credit analysis process as is used to set a derivative or foreign exchange counterparty limit or required on a corporate loan.

This analysis includes an overall assessment of the financials, credit histories, industries and management of both the counterparty and the reference credit, as well as an in-depth analysis of the reference asset involved. The result of the analysis is the assignment of a credit rating and an exposure limit. In addition to assessing the credit derivative as a new corporate loan exposure, the bank may perform marginal analysis to examine the effects of correlations between the new exposure and its existing portfolio.

Approval processes must be put in place to ensure that unscrupulous account officers do not use default swaps as a mechanism to take on unauthorised credit risk. For example, an account officer who has used his limits to emerging markets may try to conceal the true nature of his exposure by entering into a default transaction with a highly rated investment bank. In seeking approval from the credit committee, the account officer could conceal the transaction's true (emerging market) risk and present it as purely investment bank risk.

If a trading line already exists for a specific counterparty, some institutions forego fresh analysis and additional approval for the line. Other institutions prefer to set up sub-limits under the credit lines for credit derivatives. Those, however, that believe the allocation of trading products to be a business decision do not institute sub-limits.

Although a new approval may not be necessary for the counterparty's line, there is often a new and separate approval for each credit derivative transaction. If a reference credit has recently been analysed for a separate transaction, that work may be leveraged; however, before the transaction can be approved, there are still several additional analyses that should be performed.

The credit risk management function would also need to assess the volatility of the credits in question. A trader could look at the benchmark curves for Colombia and Brazil, for example, and notice that they were identical. He might potentially conclude that the pricing of both credits is also identical. This should not be the case, as the volatility of each curve is different. This fact must be assessed as part of the approval and monitoring process.

Credit derivatives have several unique attributes such that each transaction requires additional credit analysis. For example, correlation risk (between the counterparty and the reference asset) and basis risk are two factors that stand out as needing further examination.

*Correlation risk*

As we have noted, protection buyers need to consider the joint probability of default by both the protection seller and the reference credit. Defaults of certain groups of banks and certain industrial sectors may be significantly correlated. For example, protection for a loan to a construction company should not be purchased from a bank that has significant exposure to the construction industry.

Joint probability of default can be dealt with in one of two ways. Firstly, participants in the credit derivatives market can have controls that prevent the purchase of credit protection from a counterparty whose default is significantly correlated to that of the reference credit. Alternatively, they can institute a mechanism to determine a price that represents the additional risk; if the adjusted pricing cannot be obtained in the market, the transaction should not be performed with the intended counterparty.

Default correlation between the protection seller and the reference credit is difficult to observe; consequently, a quantitative approach may be difficult and its results may be doubtful. Nevertheless, the following issues should be considered in estimating joint probability of default:

- *Country of the counterparty:* it would not be appropriate to acquire protection for an emerging market loan from a bank in the same country at normal pricing levels. The joint probability of default is high. Similarly, it would be reassuring to know that the counterparty does not have a high concentration of exposure in related countries with high correlations (eg, Asia).
- *Credit quality of the counterparty:* the protection acquirer should watch carefully the evolution of the counterparty's credit quality. If the credit quality were to worsen, the joint probability of default would obviously increase. Therefore, it is necessary to have procedures in place to monitor and control the credit status of the protection provider, as well as that of the reference credit.
- *Industry concentration of the counterparty's portfolio:* if the counterparty has a high portfolio concentration in a specific industry, it may not be appropriate to buy protection from it for a corporate entity in that same industry.

*Basis risk analysis*
A perfect hedge (no basis risk) would consist of a credit derivative that is structured with the underlying asset as the reference asset. However, given the relative illiquidity of the market, a perfect hedge is not always possible. For example, a protection seller would probably be disinclined to use a loan as a reference asset, given the illiquid and private nature of loans. Therefore, a bank wanting to purchase protection for a loan exposure would have to use a more public benchmark, such as a bond, to the same reference credit.

Each transaction necessitates a careful analysis of the risks inherent in each asset, as well as their relationship to each other. Alternative reference assets should be compared against the underlying exposures for the best fit. Factors such as maturity, currency, collateral, mark-to-market valuations, seniority and liquidity should be considered. In addition, analysis should be performed to determine whether or not the credit derivative is an effective hedge for the underlying risk.

*Market risk analysis*
While the credit risk management function would consider the above analyses before approving a credit derivative transaction, the market risk management function must analyse the effects of interest rate and spread volatility on the transaction. The market risk management function may not have direct approval responsibilities; however, it must work closely with the credit risk management function to fully understand the risks inherent in each transaction. These two groups must also work hand-in-hand with the trading function when they are examining and approving new credit derivative products.

## Risk measurement and limits
Credit derivatives present some unique challenges in terms of measuring risk and calculating exposure. These challenges are due to the two sources of credit risk in a credit derivative (counterparty risk and reference credit risk), plus the need to integrate market risk and credit risk.

Systems are, of course, a critical part of the measurement process. Because of the unique qualities of credit derivatives, most derivatives and risk systems do not yet accommodate them.

*Credit risk measurement*
For the protection buyer, the credit derivative creates exposure to the protection

seller. This can be measured in the traditional way for derivatives – mark-to-market plus potential exposure – and included in exposure measurement systems. The potential exposure calculation could reach the amount of protection being purchased. The buyer also needs to consider the benefits of the hedge when measuring the credit exposure to the reference credit. The derivative creates an offset to the reference credit exposure.

For protection sellers, there is also counterparty exposure to the buyer. Again measured on a mark-to-market plus potential exposure basis, this time the calculation represents the positive value of future payments to be received from the buyer, plus a potential exposure calculation of how much the value of these future payments could change. The seller also has to measure the additional exposure of the reference credit, to the full amount of the protection sold.

Specific risk (the risk of changes in the market's perception of the creditworthiness of the reference credit) can be measured by several methodologies. Typically, specific risk is included in the VaR methodology. The probabilities of upgrades and downgrades can affect market value and should be captured in the VaR.

Credit derivatives are a new source of credit. As such, they should be linked to the bank's existing practices for credit reserves. Credit reserve methodologies can track the risk of default by both the counterparty and reference asset.

Credit risk managers normally establish limits for each counterparty and reference asset. Some limit systems allocate limits to certain business lines and products. It is common for a separate credit line to be allocated to derivatives, and sometimes particularly to credit derivatives. Maintaining a separate line for credit derivatives can be a convenient means of controlling liquidity risk. Due to their illiquid nature, it is helpful to create a separate line for credit derivatives for each counterparty. This provides a convenient means of limiting exposure and assuring diversification. Liquidity limits are typically based on notional amounts.

Measuring the bank's total exposure to each counterparty should provide for netting positions across products (where this is permitted and supported by appropriate documentation). Measuring exposure by term can be particularly important. For instance, a corporation could be long in a nine-year loan and also short in a five-year total return swap with the same counterparty. This results in a forward credit exposure of four years beginning in the fifth year.

*Market risk measurement*

The market risk measurement for credit derivatives needs to address the current value (mark-to-market) as market risk. However, due to the illiquidity of the market and the uncertainty of many models, it is often difficult to mark the derivative to market. Some instruments are transparent, while others rely on models with periodic broker/dealer quotes to support the price levels.

Market risk for credit derivatives is measured in a similar way to market risk for other derivative products. There is typically a VaR methodology and measurements of direction (delta), curve (gamma) and volatility (vega) risks. Institutions may want to consider the notional reporting of overall positions. Cashflow forecasts for the portfolio readily fit into most VaR models for interest rate risk. Analysis is required for the spread risk; this can be a separate VaR calculation, but it is significant and it may thus be desirable to incorporate the spread risk into the VaR methodology of the institution.

Market risk limits are usually set on a VaR basis. VaR can be adjusted for an appropriate holding period to reflect the illiquidity of the products (depending on the market risk measurement philosophy that is used).

## Systems

Credit derivatives are relatively new, and consequently very few commercially available systems, whether for lending, trading or risk management, adequately address their unique requirements. Most banks use internal applications, and many functions are still spreadsheet-based. The unique characteristics of credit derivatives that systems need to address include counterparty exposures, pricing models and risk models. The major problem with designing a dedicated system is that these products are far from homogeneous. The diversity of products would lead to a myriad of possible data input points (ie, input screen format difficulties), and the processing and calculation of the possibilities would represent a significant build.

One of the major current discussion points is whether credit derivatives are structured products (and should therefore be accounted, controlled and monitored as one product) or whether the cashflows should be separated out into component parts and controlled separately through the relevant systems.

Counterparty exposure systems need to be modified to account for credit derivatives. The key difference between credit derivatives and other products is that most systems are built around one transaction, one counterparty and one credit risk, while credit derivatives contain two sources of credit exposure. Exposure systems for credit derivatives need to measure both the counterparty and the reference credit exposures, yet there is only one transaction booked. In addition, exposure to the reference credit can be long and short, and this exposure needs to be combined with loan measures.

Pricing models are also different for credit derivatives. Most derivative models are based on market risk parameters, but credit derivatives include credit risk as well. The models need to reflect the probabilities and volatilities of default for different credit ratings, as well as the estimated recovery rates and expected timings of these cashflows.

Data to support these models is usually weak. In general, banks do not have adequate systems for capturing historic credit data in order to calculate future risk and probability of loss. Better systems are needed to track internal loss experience and to include data from external sources whenever possible.

Furthermore, one should be very careful about placing too much reliance on historic data. Data is scarce, and there is a continuing need for better tools to predict the future on the basis of the past. For example, information about the impact of macroeconomic factors on credit defaults might be deemed relevant and included in pricing models for credit derivatives.

Risk measurement systems also need to be modified. In the measurement discussion above, we described separate VaR models for market and credit risk. These models need to be included in reporting systems. Some institutions have taken a more ideal approach by combining market and credit risk in one VaR model.

## Risk management policies

Banks have comprehensive risk management policies covering market, credit and other risks. Policy manuals should be updated to reflect the unique attributes of credit derivatives. Specific policy considerations include the following:

- Credit derivatives are typically 'new products' and consequently need approval according to new product approval standards. Situations have arisen whereby credit derivatives have not gone through a new product approval process because their component parts have been approved in some other form. Of particular concern will be the review of pricing models and the incorporation of credit derivatives into risk measurement models and reporting.

- Limit structures will need to be updated. Credit derivatives are a separate business line, and they may require their own limits for market and counterparty risk.
- Due to the infancy of the market, many institutions require approval for individual transactions, even if they are within delegated limits. Approvals should consider risk; pricing; legal and contract issues; and suitability.
- Profit and loss reserves may need to be established to defer income recognition in light of low liquidity and pricing model uncertainty.
- All policies should be reassessed to make sure that new products are properly addressed.

## Regulatory considerations

Many credit derivative transactions are undertaken to reduce exposures and capital needs for the purpose of meeting year-end reporting requirements. Risk managers for protection buyers and sellers need to understand the regulatory impact of all types of credit derivative transactions.

Moreover, regulatory capital requirements need to be included in pricing decisions for credit derivatives, and capital requirements or benefits that are generated from credit derivative transactions should also be included in the institution's overall capital management process.

### Management reporting

The objective of reporting risk management information to management is to articulate the nature of the institution's business clearly – including a consideration of: key risks, profitability, risk/reward profiles and the impact of credit derivatives on the institution's current and future environments. The reports should be designed to help both line and senior management answer questions such as:

- Are the risks clearly understood and articulated?
- Are the risks consistent with the institution's overall strategy for business and specific risk?
- Is the business adequately compensated for these risks?
- Are there any concentrations that could impact the quality of earnings?

Effective reporting requires translating raw data into information that can support business and risk management objectives. This information needs to heighten awareness so that decisions can be based on an understanding of current and future situations. The information should be tailored to each level of management: business, trading and/or risk managers; senior management; and executive management.

- Business, trading and risk managers typically receive daily information including detailed positions (frequently at the transaction level); market and credit risk measures in comparison to limits; daily profit and loss attribution analysis; and significant market, credit or operational events.
- Senior management receives monthly information on overall risk profiles, performance, concentrations, trend analysis and market outlook.
- Executive management receives quarterly information on overall business and customer risks, risk-adjusted performance, trend analysis and the status of key initiatives.

## Conclusion

Credit derivatives present new challenges in terms of the measurement, modelling and assessment of both market and credit risk. We have discussed the inherent risks and mitigation strategies for an organisation using or trading these instruments. Credit derivatives require new approaches to quantification and place demands upon support systems. They raise new issues for fundamental credit and transaction analysis.

In the past, the introduction of new instruments has increased risk exposures and, unfortunately, has too often resulted in substantial losses when sound risk management practices were not in place. To guard against unpleasant surprises, an effective risk management process is essential. Before becoming active in this market, all potential users of credit derivatives should institute a comprehensive risk management framework that addresses the unique attributes of credit derivatives.

The authors would like to thank Rafael Cavestany, Charles Andrews and Yuri Yoshizawa for their assistance in the preparation of this chapter.

# 4

# The pricing of credit derivatives

Andreas Petrie, Klaus-Peter Schommer and Dr Ingo Schneider
Helaba Capital Markets Debt Group

## Credit risk and credit derivatives

An investor who owns a corporate bond is usually exposed to both market risk and credit risk. Market risk is related to movements in government interest rates (in our terms zero coupon rates) and spreads for a given credit quality. Credit risk in its general form evolves from the possibility of defaults and credit migration, regardless of whether an upgrade or a downgrade has occurred. Ideally market risk and credit risk should be addressed jointly because, in most cases, default or downgrading is triggered by changes in asset values and financial rates.

Therefore estimating credit risk – which includes default and credit spread risk – is a necessary prerequisite for pricing credit derivatives. Cash credit products pay a premium over default-free bonds. The premium or credit spread is mainly determined by the market's credit risk evaluation. Credit derivatives are used to provide protection against credit risk shifts and counterparty default.

Currently the pricing of cash credit products is based on market information, personal experience and instinct. Traders and investors know at which level a credit is currently traded. There is often a common idea of the underlying market value. In addition, people have their own views on particular sectors and risks. This leads especially for liquid bonds to an efficient trading market. In contrast, the markets for loans are much less developed. In Germany, for example, there is no mark-to-market revaluation for loans. Loans are meant to be held to maturity. Credit risk pricing there is based more on instinct and the banks' internal risk ratings of their assets.

In practice, the means of pricing swap credit derivatives is often similar to the methodology used in the cash market. Factors beyond cash credit risks that influence the price of a given credit derivative product are additionally recognised and estimated from the trader's or bank's point of view in terms of loan or bond portfolios. In the pricing of forward risk and credit spread options, it is necessary to use an acceptable and practicable model, but for the time being no general accepted model exists. Currently, market participants are a long way from having a model comparable to the overall accepted interest rate option models. However, a great deal of effort is being made to establish tools that take advantage of existing procedures.

Since the mid-1970s, steps have been taken towards developing mathematical models for the pricing of credit risk. The oldest approaches are firm valuation models. Here default bonds are viewed as contingent claims on the firm's value. The value of the firm follows a diffusion process (ie, a statistical process that is overlaid by random noise). Its movements are the determining factor in the corporate's bond prices. The pricing follows the well known option price theory. Firm value models were originally set up for the valuation of defaultable bonds and can also be used to price derivatives on defaultable bonds. But pricing such a derivative requires a calibration process where the prices of the bond and the derivative are calculated simultaneously. This is one of the disadvantages of firm value models for pricing credit derivatives, as it would be preferable for the price of the underlying to be an input parameter for the pricing of the derivative. Another problem with such models is their inability to handle credit spread options.

In a more recent approach, so-called intensity models became popular. Intensity-based models are able to value default and spread option products. They use a Poisson process such as an unpredictable environment to describe default, capturing the idea that the timing of defaults takes the bondholders by surprise. In order to implement a Poisson process, a Monte Carlo simulation or a term structure model in combination with exogenous parameters is used. Intensity models are becoming successful pricing tools.

It should be noted that the difference between the firm valuation approach and intensity-based models is not very clear. Usually models that use the value of the firm can easily be intensity-based by describing the value of the firm as a jump process.

On the other hand the intensity-based models could easily incorporate the value of the firm by using it as a variable affecting the default intensity.

## Pricing a default swap

The value of a defaultable product's credit risk takes into account the market's estimation of its default probability and recovery rate. Besides other factors such as liquidity, tradability and funding levels, default probability and recovery rate are the main components of credit spreads. Because the cash credit product and the related default swap are exposed to the same credit risk, it is very clear that in a traditional pricing framework the credit spread of the underlying is the major parameter for the pricing of a default swap.

An investor in a defaultable asset receives a positive spread compared with an investor in a default-free bond, according to the market's evaluation of the credit risk to which he is exposed. This position can be synthetically created by buying a default-free bond and selling insurance to the market with the defaultable asset as the reference asset. This simple reflection shows the relationship between the cash products and the derivatives prices. However, they do not correspond because in reality other factors besides default probability and recovery rate determine the prices of cash credit products and default swaps.

Such factors in the pricing of default swaps include the counterparty's risk provision and capital costs, which are more important in the context of credit derivatives pricing than when they relate to interest rate derivatives. For a buyer of insurance, the real level of protection depends on the ability of the insurance seller to fulfil its payment in the event of a default on the underlying security. Buying protection from a AAA-rated insurer should therefore be more expensive than buying from a BBB-rated institution. Selling protection also requires taking the rating of the counterparty into account, as the seller must replace the insurance short position in event of a default by the protection buyer.

Ideally protection with a default swap wholly covers the loss occurring from the default on the security. This is only true if the defaultable security and the reference asset correspond. Often there is a difference in the risk profile between the risk to be insured and the reference security. Therefore a buyer of protection needs to choose a reference asset with a risk close to that of the security to be insured. Factors that affect the basic risk between the reference asset and the asset to be secured are tenor, currency, seniority, and – above all – the issuer's creditworthiness. The implication for pricing is that the more a reference asset features a liquid and tradable asset of a particular issuer, the less the premium rises and vice versa.

Market breadth and depth rely on market efficiency and fair prices. The result of a lack of market breadth and depth is a spread rise. The credit risks currently hedgable with default swaps are limited and the number of market participants is often not yet big enough to get fair two-way prices. The economic crisis in East Asia has made this obvious. On the other hand, for many liquid risks a default swap market has been established. Here prices become fair and show a common idea of the default swap's value, just as in the traditional valuation of cash products. This process will continue because of the rapidly growing market interest in credit derivatives.

The fast-growing market for credit derivatives is also being affected by the many investigations into practicable mathematical pricing models by financial engineers who are able to price more complex credit derivatives such as credit spread options. Over the longer term these models will also affect the traditional pricing framework of cash credit products, which might lead to a mark-to-market revaluation of banks' cash loan portfolios and an efficient trading market for loans. This is a big challenge for banks' portfolio managers, who are used to leaving loans booked with the original price until an accountant demands a depreciation.

Helaba is currently in the process of implementing a pricing tool based on an intensity model for default swaps and credit spread options. In the following sections, we have demonstrated the basic means of pricing a default swap within an intensity model framework and pricing a simple credit spread option.

## Pricing procedures

### Pricing a credit default swap

In a credit default swap one party receives a fixed stream of payments in return for which it pays nothing unless the underlying bond defaults. This is like an insurance contract protecting the holder of the underlying from the consequences of default.

Usually the value of default is not affected directly by changes in the riskless interest rate or by changes in credit spreads. We assume that only the probability of default matters.

In the following example, the default methods determine the price of a credit derivative as the expected loss resulting from default, which is calculated from estimations of the default probability and recovery rate. The default probability is approximated by using the security's rating. To estimate the default probability over time, it is possible to use credit rating transition matrices such as those published by rating agencies. A transition matrix is a simple square matrix depicting the probability in one period of a security's migrating from any given credit rating to another, including the possibility of default. In the following example, the matrix is a simplified version of an original published by Standard and Poor's:

$$P = \begin{pmatrix} 0.85 & 0.10 & 0.05 \\ 0.15 & 0.75 & 0.10 \\ 0.00 & 0.00 & 1.00 \end{pmatrix} \begin{matrix} \to A \\ \to B \\ \to D \end{matrix}$$

There are three credit states: (A, B, D). Class A denotes the highest credit rating, Class B represents the lower credit rating and Class D indicates a state of default. The matrix contains the probabilities of a rating changing from one state to another over a given period. Reading the numbers in the first row, it is possible to see the three possible levels that a Class A rating can follow. For instance, it remains in Class A (a probability of 0.85), it changes to rating Class B (a probability of 0.10) or it goes into default, or Class D, (a probability of 0.05). Class B may upgrade to Class A (a probability of 0.15), remain as Class B (a probability of 0.75) or default (a probability of 0.1).

Class D is a special state that assumes that once this level is reached, the system will remain in default.

Generally speaking, for each of these three states the market assigns maturity-specific spreads over the risk-free rate at which risky bonds are traded.

For further calculations, we assume a recovery rate (denoted as $\eta$), which is fixed. Furthermore, we assume that the recovery amount in the event of default is received at the maturity of the underlying instrument. These are the main ingredients of a model published by Jarrow-Lando-Turnbull (JLT),[1] which characterises bankruptcy as a Markov process in the firm's credit rating.

To simplify the calculations further we assume a given term structure of default-free bonds, a given term structure of spreads for each rating class (A and B) and, as mentioned above, a constant recovery rate. As in JLT, any correlation between interest rates and the default process is ignored.

So far we have found statistical default probabilities based upon historical estimations in our matrix, $P$. But in order to price a credit derivative, we need to find risk-neutral default probabilities and to use them in conjunction with a term structure model. So it is necessary to convert the statistical probabilities into risk-neutral probabilities using a so-called risk adjustment.

The example below covers two periods:

The riskless zero coupon rate is given as $r(t) = 0.0525 - 0.0519 \cdot e^{-0.22 \cdot t}$, which closely resembles the Libor curve for Deutschmarks as of mid-June 1998.

So we write the riskless zero rates for two periods as a vector:

$$r = \begin{pmatrix} 0.0397 \\ 0.0423 \end{pmatrix}$$

The spot rate is 0.0397 in the first period and 0.0423 in the second period, assuming that spreads given for our two risky classes are as follows:

$$S_A = \begin{pmatrix} 0.010 \\ 0.015 \end{pmatrix} \qquad S_B = \begin{pmatrix} 0.015 \\ 0.020 \end{pmatrix}$$

For the bond in Class A we assume a spread of 0.010 for the first period, compared to the riskless term structure and a spread of 0.015 for the second period.

Furthermore our recovery rate is constant with a value of $\eta = 0.6$.

At maturity the bond will be in one of the three states: (A, B, D). If the bond ends in the first two states, then the pay-off on the zero coupon bond will be 1. In the event of default, it ends up with a pay-off of $\eta$. Therefore we define a cashflow vector for all of these states thus:

[1] R. Jarrow, D. Lando and S. Turnbull, 'A Markov model for the term structure of credit spreads', *Review of Financial Studies*, vol. 10, pp.481–523 (1997).

$$C = \begin{pmatrix} 1 \\ 1 \\ \eta \end{pmatrix}$$

Hence our procedure is as follows:
1. Calculate risk-neutral default probabilities.
2. Use a term structure model to discount back the cashflows in the event of default.

### Calculating risk-neutral default probabilities

In order to calculate the risk-neutral probabilities, we multiply the off-diagonal elements by an adjustment denoted as $\pi$. For our bond currently in Class $A$, the chances of ending the first period at the various ratings are as follows:

$$P_A = \begin{pmatrix} 0.85 \\ 0.01 \\ 0.05 \end{pmatrix}$$

To transform this into a risk-neutral vector $R_A$ with the risk adjustment $\pi_A$:

$$R_A = \begin{pmatrix} 1 - (1 - 0.85)\pi_A \\ 0.10\pi_A \\ 0.05\pi_A \end{pmatrix}$$

To solve this and determine our necessary risk adjustment, we will find the value of $\pi_A$ that makes the expected value of discounted cashflows equal to the traded price of our Class $A$ bond and satisfies our well known no-arbitrage condition:

$$B_A(1) = C^T \cdot R_A$$

$$\frac{1}{1 + r(1) + S_A(1)} = \frac{1}{1 + r(1)} \cdot [1 \ 1 \ \eta] \cdot \begin{bmatrix} 1 - (1 - 0.85)\pi_A \\ 0.10\pi_A \\ 0.05\pi_A \end{bmatrix}$$

This equation can be solved analytically. The risk adjustment for the $n$th period for a security initially in state $i$ ($i = A$ or $B$) can be written

$$\pi_i(n) = \left[ 1 - \left( \frac{1 + r(n)}{1 + r(n) + S_i(n)} \right)^n \right] \cdot \frac{1}{(1 - \eta) \cdot P_{di}(n)}$$

where $P_{di}(n)$ is the cumulative probability of a state of default over $n$ periods initially in state $i$ (the last entry in each row of the transition matrix). This derivation makes it easy to calculate the necessary numbers for the adjustments.
For example in the first period we get:

$$\pi_A(1) = \left[ 1 - \left( \frac{1 + 0.0397}{1 + 0.0397 + 0.010} \right)^1 \right] \cdot \frac{1}{(1 - 0.6) \cdot 0.05} = 0.4763$$

$$\pi_B(1) = \left[ 1 - \left( \frac{1 + 0.0397}{1 + 0.0397 + 0.015} \right)^1 \right] \cdot \frac{1}{(1 - 0.6) \cdot 0.1} = 0.3555$$

Using these numbers, we obtain the risk-adjusted matrix for the first period:

$$R(1) = \begin{pmatrix} 0.9286 & 0.0476 & 0.0238 \\ 0.0533 & 0.9111 & 0.0356 \\ 0.00 & 0.00 & 1.00 \end{pmatrix}$$

To proceed further, we calculate the risk adjustment for the second period. However, first we have to derive the transition matrix for the second period, which is just a matrix multiplication of the transition matrix for the first period:

$$P(2) = P \cdot P = P^2$$

$$= \begin{bmatrix} 0.85 & 0.10 & 0.05 \\ 0.15 & 0.75 & 0.10 \\ 0.00 & 0.00 & 1.00 \end{bmatrix} \times \begin{bmatrix} 0.85 & 0.10 & 0.05 \\ 0.15 & 0.75 & 0.10 \\ 0.00 & 0.00 & 1.00 \end{bmatrix}$$

$$= \begin{bmatrix} 0.7375 & 0.1600 & 0.1025 \\ 0.2400 & 0.5775 & 0.1825 \\ 0.00 & 0.00 & 1.00 \end{bmatrix}$$

Proceeding as above, for the risk adjustment factors in the second period we obtain:

$$\pi_A(2) = \left[ 1 - \left( \frac{1 + 0.0423}{1 + 0.0423 + 0.015} \right)^2 \right] \cdot \frac{1}{(1 - 0.6) \cdot 0.1025} = 0.6872$$

$$\pi_B(2) = \left[ 1 - \left( \frac{1 + 0.0423}{1 + 0.0423 + 0.020} \right)^2 \right] \cdot \frac{1}{(1 - 0.6) \cdot 0.1825} = 0.5110$$

So with this adjustment calculation we get $R(2)$ as:

$$R(2) = \begin{pmatrix} 0.8196 & 0.1099 & 0.0704 \\ 0.1226 & 0.7841 & 0.0932 \\ 0.00 & 0.00 & 1.00 \end{pmatrix}$$

Since this simple methodology described above models explicitly the event of default, we can price a default swap without difficulty. For instance, in order to price a default swap, we multiply the cumulative probability of default by the loss on default and discount it back with the interest rate for two periods.

That means for our Class $A$ swap value:

$$SWAP_D = \frac{0.0704 \cdot (1 - 0.6)}{(1 + 0.0423)^2} = 0.0259$$

This produces a reduction in the present value of the swap of 0.0259.

On the other hand, the value of a risky bond is the difference between a risk-free bond and the default value. In our case, this is the difference between a riskless zero coupon bond and the risky two-year zero coupon bond:

$$P_{Risky} = \frac{100}{(1 + 0.0423)^2} - \frac{100 \cdot 0.0704 \cdot (1 - 0.6)}{(1 + 0.0423)^2} = 92.048 - 2.592 = 89.456$$

So compared with a default-free bond, the value of a risky bond is reduced by about 2.59 units.

### Using a term structure model

Any term structure model can be used in order to price credit derivatives, and we will use a trinomial representation of the Black-Karasinski model. This model has lognormal interest rates and has the property of mean reversion.

The stochastic process for the spot rate is given in the model[2]

$$d\ln r = \left((\Theta(t) - a\ln r)dt + \sigma dz\right)$$

where $a$ and $\sigma$ are given constants and simplify the original Black-Karasinski model somewhat for our purposes (in the original model, Black-Karasinski have made these two parameters time-dependent). The above equation describes mathematically the evolution of the spot rate as lognormal interest rates, which is widely accepted by practitioners. $\Theta(t)$ is a function of time and ensures that the model fits the initial term structure (eg, zero coupon rates), whereas $\sigma$ is the instantaneous standard deviation of the short rate and $a$ is the parameter that pulls the rate to its expected value.

In Exhibit 4.1 we illustrate how the interest rate tree evolves over a period of two years with our initially given spot rate $r(t)$ and the two constants $a = 0.1$ and $\sigma = 0.25$. Steps of one year are used.

In this trinomial tree each node has three branches with three different probabilities at each node. The fact that at nodes E and I the tree doesn't spread out any more is due to the inclusion of mean reversion in the calculations.

In Exhibit 4.2 we combine all the necessary information to value a security.[3] If we value our risky security within the tree, we will get the same difference in price as shown in the simple calculation above.

---

[2] J. Hull and A. White, 'Numerical procedures for implementing term structure models I: single factor models', *The Journal of Derivatives* 2, New York, 1 pp.7–16 (1994).

[3] Note that we are dealing here with continuous compounded interest rates but this should not change our results.

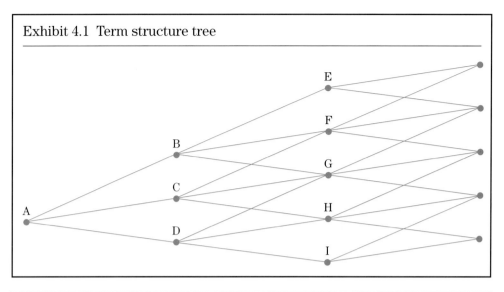

Exhibit 4.1  Term structure tree

Exhibit 4.2  Rates and risk free probabilities of trinomial tree

| Node | A | B | C | D | E | F | G | H | I |
|------|-----|-----|-----|-----|-----|-----|-----|-----|-----|
| Rate | 0.0397 | 0.0670 | 0.0435 | 0.0282 | 0.1092 | 0.0708 | 0.0459 | 0.0298 | 0.0193 |
| Pup | 0.167 | 0.122 | 0.167 | 0.222 | 0.887 | 0.122 | 0.167 | 0.222 | 0.087 |
| Pmd | 0.666 | 0.656 | 0.666 | 0.656 | 0.026 | 0.656 | 0.666 | 0.656 | 0.026 |
| Pdn | 0.167 | 0.222 | 0.167 | 0.122 | 0.087 | 0.222 | 0.167 | 0.122 | 0.887 |

*Source:* Helaba.

At the end of the life of the bond – ie, two years (nodes E, F, G, H and I) – we must subtract the cumulative probability of default provided from our previous analysis, multiplied by the loss on default from our riskless zero coupon bond, which gives a price of

$$P_{nodes} = 100 - 0.0704 \cdot (1 - 0.6) = 97.184$$

at each of these nodes (the bond has a notional value of 100). In order to get the price as of today, we have to roll back through the tree as follows. At node B we calculate the risky bond value using the probabilities from Exhibit 4.2 together with the node values in the second year:

$$P_{node\,B} = e^{(-0.067 \cdot 1)} \cdot (0.122 \cdot 97.184 + 0.656 \cdot 97.184 + 0.222 \cdot 97.184)$$

$$= 90.88$$

Similarly we get for node C and D values of 93.05 and 94.48 respectively. Finally, we get a value of 89.308 for our risky two-year bond. Compared with a price of 91.88, which is our price for a two-year zero coupon bond, this again reflects a difference of 2.59, as shown above.

One main drawback of this procedure is that we must assume that riskless rates are uncorrelated with default and therefore that the given credit spreads are uncorrelated with interest rates, which contradicts practical experience. Furthermore we have assumed that cashflows in the event of default are received at maturity and not at the time of default.

To overcome these problems Das-Tufano[4] extended this approach and added some more realistic assumptions to the JLT approach. They describe the recovery rates as a stochastic variable and make the term structure of interest rates correlate with the recovery rate. They also take into account the possibility that when a security defaults, the recovered amount is soon paid out. In their terms, we then have to calculate so-called first passage time probabilities. A general way of implementing such a procedure is to use a two-factor approach, but this goes beyond the scope of this chapter.

## Pricing a credit spread option

Credit spread options are written on the final value of credit spreads over a given time horizon. An option may be written, for example, such that it pays out when the spread exceeds a pre-defined threshold value after a fixed time (eg, two years). Spreads are affected both by default and by variations in spreads prior to default. Their option-like nature makes them accessible to the well known option pricing techniques using trees, as we will show.

For calculation purposes we also assume that the spread process follows a mean reverting process and can be described in a similar way to our term structure above. We assume a term structure of spreads given as market values as follows:

$$Spread = \begin{pmatrix} 0.010 \\ 0.015 \\ 0.020 \end{pmatrix}$$

So the spread in one year's time is 0.010 over the one-year zero rate. In the second year, the spread is 0.015 over the zero rate, and so on. Again, the necessary parameters for our tree calculations for the spread are given as $a = 0.1$ and $\sigma = 0.04$.

The results for the spreads are shown in Exhibit 4.3. The risk-neutral probabilities can again be taken from Exhibit 4.2.

We will now price a two-year call spread option struck at 2.5 per cent. At the end of the option's maturity, we have to apply the condition:

$$Opt_{node\ i} = MAX(Spread(i, j) - Strike, 0)$$

So we have at node E a value of 0.0344–0.025 = 0.0094; at node F a value of 0.0071, calculated in a similar fashion; at node G a value of 0.005; and finally at nodes H and I, J we have values of 0.003 and 0.0011 respectively. Now we move backwards in the tree and use the information from Exhibit 4.2.

---

### Exhibit 4.3 Spread value at the nodes of the trinomial tree

| Node | A | B | C | D | E | F | G | H | I |
|------|------|--------|------|--------|--------|--------|------|-------|--------|
| Spread | 0.01 | 0.0214 | 0.02 | 0.0186 | 0.0344 | 0.0321 | 0.03 | 0.028 | 0.0261 |

*Source:* Helaba.

---

[4] S. Das and P. Tufano, 'Pricing credit sensitive debt when interest rates, credit ratings and credit spreads are stochastic', *Journal of Financial Engineering*, vol. 5, pp.161–198 (1996).

At node B we have:

$$Opt_{node\,B} = e^{-0.067} \cdot (0.122 \cdot 0.0094 + 0.656 \cdot 0.0071 + 0.222 \cdot 0.005) = 0.00646$$

At node C we calculate a value of:

$$Opt_{node\,C} = e^{-0.0435} \cdot (0.167 \cdot 0.0071 + 0.666 \cdot 0.005 + 0.167 \cdot 0.001) = 0.0048$$

And at the last node in the first year, the value of the option is:

$$Opt_{node\,D} = e^{-0.0282} \cdot (0.222 \cdot 0.005 + 0.656 \cdot 0.003 + 0.122 \cdot 0.0011) = 0.0031$$

So finally we discount the values at these nodes back to today and get:

$$Opt_{node\,A} = e^{-0.0397} \cdot (0.167 \cdot 0.00646 + 0.666 \cdot 0.0048 + 0.167 \cdot 0.0031) = 0.0046$$

The value of the option is 0.46 per cent, or 46 bps.

Usually these simple calculations have to be extended to more periods to give a more accurate price. This step is straightforward, however, and does not affect the methodology.

## Summary

We have shown in this short overview some basic pricing techniques concerning the valuation of credit derivatives. This overview is by no means complete. The examples presented here were on the intensity model. There is no doubt that the firm valuation approach for pricing credit derivatives is also important. Therefore, careful examination of other possible choices should be undertaken before making any decision as to the kind of pricing approach that should be used.

# 5

# The convergence of the trading environment with the credit department

Mark Gheerbrant
Rabobank International

## Introduction

The title of this chapter suggests that a process of change is taking place in the functions of either trading or credit departments, or possibly both. This is certainly the case in most banks, where there are two main drivers of change. Firstly the development of new products, particularly in the areas of credit derivatives and securitisation, is aiding the creation of a more liquid market in credit risk. This will allow credit risk to be more actively managed than has been possible in the past. Secondly, many of the advanced analytical techniques developed in the interest rate market for pricing complex options are now being applied to the credit markets. Models for calculating the 'risk' in a portfolio using objective quantitative analysis are now readily available to credit managers, which will potentially radically change the way they view risk.

While these are the major drivers of change, there are also other factors involved, particularly the provisions in the latest Capital Adequacy Directives which permit the use of internal risk models to calculate regulatory capital requirements.

Each of these factors will be examined in more detail in this chapter, together with their likely impact on both credit and trading departments. Possible future developments will also be assessed to see whether current trends are likely to continue.

## The current role of the credit department

The primary role of the credit department in a bank is to manage the bank's credit exposures across its whole product range. This will include, among other things:

- performing credit research on specific companies, sectors or countries;
- setting the amount of exposure the organisation is prepared to take on an entity (in conjunction with credit committees) and allocating this to various areas of the bank; and
- measuring the bank's actual exposures to companies, sectors or countries and monitoring these against the set limits.

This is, of course, something of an oversimplification and the credit department has many other functions, including establishing policies for how credit risk is quantified and setting procedures for credit approval. Credit departments vary enormously among banks in terms of their levels of sophistication, but in general they have various characteristics in common, including the following:

- The credit analysis that is performed is based on analysing the economics of the company or country involved. To this extent it is highly subjective. Even where credit scoring systems are used to determine the permitted exposure, the systems themselves are subjective.
- Credit departments tend to adopt a passive approach to credit risk management. Although credit limits will be increased or decreased over time, once an exposure is taken on it is generally left until maturity.
- As a result of the passive approach and the assumption that exposures will be held until maturity, credit departments look only at the default risk element of credit risk and entirely ignore the market risk element.
- Most credit departments do not generally 'charge' users of credit limits for the lines they utilise. This is not universally true, but where banks do charge users it tends to be on a basis of probability of loss.

It is worth noting at this point that the credit department only manages the bank's credit exposures, it does not control them. Credit risk will arise as a result of just about every activity of the bank, and the only control that the credit department has is to limit the maximum exposures.

## The role of the trading department

Several years ago credit trading departments were really bond trading departments, the primary role of which was to underwrite and distribute fairly plain vanilla debt instruments. Secondary market trading activity was also required to provide liquidity to the investors. Although these activities are still important, the advent of new products has meant that trading departments have evolved to act as warehouses for credit risk. They take on credit exposure in a variety of forms, including bonds, loans, participations and derivatives and seek to sell the credit risk to investors at a higher price than they paid for it. In some cases the credit exposure is sold in the same form in which it is acquired, and in other cases it may be restructured by asset swapping, repackaging, securitisation or using credit derivatives.

To some extent the trading department of a bank has greater ability to control the credit exposures it takes on than the credit department, but it will still have to accept some risks that it would not otherwise choose as a result of doing business. To this extent, it has just as much a risk management function as the credit department. Of course, as a part of any trading operation there will be a proprietary trading function, and here credit risk is taken on solely with a view to making profit out of the change in value of the credit over time. In most trading operations, however, this is currently a relatively small part of the overall credit trading business.

The trading department will generally adopt a different view of credit risk management from the credit department:

- While credit analysis is performed, the emphasis is much more on the price at which the exposure is acquired. This is still generally based on a market price approach, although theoretical modelling is being used increasingly for more complex credit derivatives.

- The trading department will adopt a much more active approach towards risk management, with exposures being increased or decreased on a daily basis and short positions in credit being taken at times.
- As a result of the short-term view, the trading department will look much more at the market risk element of credit risk (ie, the change in value of a position due to a change in the credit spread) and will generally take little notice of the default risk element.

It is apparent from the very brief look at the roles of the two departments that, although they are both dealing with the credit risk, they are looking at it and managing it in very different ways. This is typically reflected in limit structures. Credit departments generally set limits in terms of maximum nominal exposure to a particular entity, whereas trading departments generally have some type of market risk limit, possibly based on value at risk (VaR), reflecting the maximum loss from given market movements.

The next step, therefore, is to examine whether these differences in approach are likely to change due to the developments in analytical techniques and the arrival of credit derivatives.

## The impact of credit derivatives

In most banks, credit limits are a scarce resource and, together with capital, can be a significant constraint on developing business. Despite this, in many organisations they are not used efficiently. Certain departments may be given limits that they do not utilise, while other areas of the bank may have insufficient limits to the same counterparties to operate effectively. In many banks there is no mechanism for ensuring that scarce limits are allocated to the area that can use them most profitably. Many of these problems arise because users of lines are not charged. With the development of the credit derivatives market, this becomes much easier to change.

Probably the main purpose of credit derivatives is to create a standard and simple mechanism by which credit risk can be both bought and, more importantly, sold, thereby creating a liquid market in credit risk. A corollary of this is that it is also possible to price any credit risk. The market is already sufficiently liquid for this to apply to some credits, particularly sovereign risk, and it is reasonable to assume that it will apply to all credits once the market matures. This will have a profound effect on the way banks operate, by making it much easier to assess whether returns by customer or by country are sufficient to justify the allocation of the credit limit.

Consider a bank that is prepared to take a US$100 million, five-year exposure to Greece. The credit department can either allocate this limit to, for example, the bond trading and trade finance groups, or alternatively sell protection on Greece in the default swaps market at, say, 50 bps per annum for five years. If the bond trading and trade finance departments do not make a net profit of US$5 million per annum, the latter course would be optimal in terms purely of revenue for the bank. In fact, given that the credit department can effectively 'sell' the bank's limit in the market, it can now easily justify charging the users of the limit 50 bps per annum. This will force businesses to assess whether they are generating sufficient returns on the risk taken.

Now consider the example of a bank contemplating lending to a manufacturing company in Greece at, say, 75 bps per annum. Since this also uses up the country limit for Greece, the incremental revenue for taking on the risk of the corporate is only 25 bps. The net return on lending to an equivalent credit quality manufacturer in, for example, Holland would be much higher. This type of analysis will effectively discourage banks from lending to companies in riskier countries and hence, over time, force up the cost of funding for these borrowers.

This process can be taken even further if one considers the example of a bank that has fully used its limit for a given country or company. The credit department can now easily go into the market and buy default protection on Greece in order to increase its limit, which it can then sell on to the relevant department. By the same token, if a limit is unused or partially used, rather than leaving it unused, the credit department can sell it in the market. Also, if a bank has a fully used limit but wishes to reduce its exposure to the entity, it can now do this immediately by buying protection rather than having to wait for exposures to mature.

This scenario is not difficult to imagine and is, in fact, already happening in some institutions. For the first time, credit departments are becoming active managers of credit risk with the ability to control the amount of exposure to credit risks, and hence the potential losses, rather than passively limiting it to a maximum. They can also become direct revenue generators for the first time. This does not mean, of course, additional revenue for the bank, but a reallocation that should more accurately reflect both the contribution from merely taking credit risk and the added value of product areas.

All of the above are clearly sensible uses of a new product that allows credit departments to undertake their activities more effectively, but does not fundamentally change their role. Once credit departments start charging for limits, however, it is a big temptation for credit officers to try to increase revenues by 'playing the markets'. If a credit officer has a view that a particular credit is deteriorating, he may try and 'buy' excess limits now with a view to 'selling' it either internally or externally at a higher margin after a few months. Clearly at this point the role of the credit department has changed from management to speculation, which, as was discussed earlier, is generally the province of the trading area and requires a different attitude towards credit risk.

Of course now the credit department has the flexibility to control exposures, it has the potential to construct diversified portfolios. This, however, requires a more quantitative approach to analysing credit risk, discussed below.

## Portfolio credit risk modelling

As mentioned previously, much of the credit analysis performed by credit departments has been subjective analysis of individual entities. This, together with relationship-based banking, has led to many banks specialising in certain areas. Rabobank is a prime example of this, having been historically a food and agricultural lender and specialising more recently in healthcare and telecommunications. Credit departments became 'expert' in analysing certain sectors, causing large sector risk concentrations to build up in lending portfolios. This is, of course, entirely contrary to the portfolio theory of risk reduction through diversification.

The development of the credit derivatives market has led to the application of more quantitative analysis techniques – many derived from the pricing of interest rate derivatives – being applied to the measurement and pricing of credit risk. Several models are now available in the market for this purpose and they are forcing credit departments to reassess the way they measure risk. These models attempt to measure the cost of counterparty default, combined with the probability of default, in order to come up with an expected loss figure. This will only be a meaningful number if it is applied to a whole portfolio. The probability of default will depend upon the riskiness of the credit, and in most models the rating is used as a proxy for this. Using historic recovery rates for different instruments and classes of debt, historic default rates for different ratings bands, and historic ratings transition matrices, it is possible to calculate expected losses of a credit portfolio over a given period of time. It is unlikely, however, that all the credits within a portfolio will be independent of each other, so it would not be correct simply to aggregate the expected loss of each individual credit exposure. The models therefore need to be able to take account of correlations between each of the credits. This will lead to greater risk in highly concentrated portfolios than in diversified portfolios, which suggests that, once this type of modelling becomes accepted, many banks will need either to alter their sector specialist approach or to find a way of managing it.

The models discussed above, however, only take account of default risk. A similar analytical approach can be used for measuring the risk within a trading portfolio, but this would also need to take account of market risk. The market risk of a credit position is essentially the risk that the value of the position will change due to a change in the credit spread (over the risk-free rate) at which the credit trades. This is itself a function of:

- idiosyncratic risk (ie, changes in the credit spread due to general market movements not related to the specific credit); and
- event risk (ie, changes in the credit spread due to an event such as the downgrading of the credit rating).

In order to model market risk, the positions are divided into buckets – generally by rating, geographic region and sector. Scenario analysis can then be performed by changing the risk factors that affect the value of the portfolio for each bucket (in this case, primarily the credit spread). The scenario sets can be generated either by using historic data or by Monte Carlo simulation. Alternatively, a specific scenario – for example, an 'Asian Flu' scenario – can be constructed for the portfolio.

## Internal risk models for capital

It is now permissible for some banks to use internal risk models to assess the regulatory capital requirement for credit portfolios. The models will be along the lines described in the previous sector, and in general they will need to take account of all the elements of credit risk – ie, idiosyncratic risk, event risk, default risk and liquidity risk. The models and the data inputs will require the approval of the relevant regulator. This change will have some interesting ramifications:

- Credit departments will be obliged to use more analytical risk measurement techniques either as well as, or instead of, more traditional credit analysis.
- Since the models will include the effects of portfolio diversification, banks with highly concentrated portfolios will be penalised in terms of the amount of capital required.
- The incremental capital required for an additional credit will depend on the credit's correlation with the existing portfolio. This means that the incremental risk and the capital required will vary from one bank to another for the same credit and hence the required return will be different for each bank.

- Credit departments will be forced to become much more active in their management of credit risk, selling credits where concentrations exist and buying credits to improve diversification. Given the different return requirements mentioned above, it should be possible for banks to swap credits in a mutually beneficial manner. This will have a major impact on the volumes of credit derivatives transacted.

The use of these models and the more active management of credit portfolios will again mean that the activities of credit departments will become more similar to those of trading departments.

## The future

The changes in products and analytical techniques that are taking place raise many possibilities regarding the way in which trading and credit departments might change further in the future. Since it is difficult to predict what might happen, some of the possibilities are raised as questions, below:

### Should quantitative analysis replace subjective credit analysis?

Most of the credit risk models being developed attempt to predict the future from the past. In other words, expected losses are based on historic default and recovery rates, which are input as a function of rating. Risk figures are therefore produced without any individual analysis of the credits involved. Will managing a portfolio on this basis produce lower losses than traditional credit analysis? Only time will tell. Of course, it is possible to combine the two approaches. A bank may wish to conduct its own analysis and use its own internal credit rating, rather than that of a rating agency. It would then also need to use its own historic default and recovery rates.

### Should credit departments have VaR limits?

Trading departments generally have VaR limits that seek to predict the losses within certain confidence levels. If banks and regulators believe this is a sound approach, why should it not be used for a bank's entire credit portfolio? Fundamentally a credit risk is just as risky whether it is in a trading book or a banking book, it is just the accounting treatment which is different. So why are different risk measures generally used?

### Should the trading department manage all the bank's exposures?

As mentioned above, credit departments will probably be forced to become more dynamic in their management of risk, buying and selling credits more actively. Such activity, however, is traditionally the domain of the trading department, so should it not be this area that performs this function? If this were to be the case, the role of the credit department would be confined to developing and validating models, collecting historic data and setting total risk limits for the bank, but on a portfolio risk basis rather than a counterparty limit basis.

## Conclusion

As we have seen, many of the techniques used by trading and credit departments to analyse credit risk have traditionally been different. Changes in products, particularly the arrival of credit derivatives, and the application of more advanced analytical techniques to credit risk management are changing the way both areas operate and bringing them closer together. Credit derivatives allow credit departments to manage risk actively for the first time, which is allowing them to look at risk on a portfolio basis rather than as a series of individual exposures. It is also affecting time horizons, as exposures can be sold if necessary. This means that market risk caused by credit spread movement needs to be taken into account, as well as default risk. These developments are also allowing credit departments to charge users of credit limits accurately, allowing them to become centres of revenue if not profit.

The use of internal risk models for regulatory capital allocation will require credit departments to focus on diversification and, interestingly, will result in each bank pricing the same credit differently.

Although the credit and trading departments are converging, it should be noted that the objectives of the two areas remain fundamentally different. Essentially, the role of the trading department is to generate revenue from the underwriting, restructuring and distribution of credit risk. This includes taking on credit risk for no other reason than to profit from changes in its value.

The fundamental role of the credit department, on the other hand, is to measure, allocate and manage the credit exposures that result directly from the bank's activities across its whole product range. Its overriding aim should therefore be to keep the organisation's credit exposures, however these are measured, within the limits that have been set by the board of directors.

While the credit department could become a revenue centre, its objective would still be to maximise revenue through the use of the limits that have been set.

The material contained in this chapter is not intended to provide specific advice on any matter and is not intended to be comprehensive. No responsibility for any loss occasioned to any person relying on material contained in this chapter will be accepted by the author, his employer or the publishers.

# 6

# Event risk management and arbitrage: synthetic credit structures

David K.A. Mordecai
Fitch IBCA, Inc.

## The diversification, pooling and transfer of credit risk via credit-linked investment vehicles

Credit-linked notes (CLNs) are exotic debt securities issued by an investment-grade entity with conventional coupon, maturity and redemption features, similar to traditional notes or bonds. A CLN differs from a more conventional debt instrument in that, by design, the performance of the CLN is dependent on the performance of a pre-specified reference asset. In this way credit risk can be unbundled and traded separately from interest rate or price volatility. CLNs achieve this redistribution of credit risk by incorporating a credit derivative into the structure of the note. Unlike traditional credit issuance, where credit risk remains irrevocably linked with the asset of its original issuance, credit derivatives permit the segregation and restructuring of the credit risk of an underlying financial instrument.

CLNs, as a special class of synthetic securities or structured notes, use the set of bankruptcy-remote mechanisms that are common to the asset-backed securities (ABS) market. These structures were developed in secondary market sales of mortgages and trade claims (inventory and receivables) sales, and in the non-recourse financing of stand-alone projects, sale/lease-backs, leveraged leases and recapitalisations, and leveraged buy-outs (LBOs). As an asset class, credit-linked investment vehicles provide access, at lower transaction costs, to both investment and risk management opportunities, for investors and hedgers seeking to achieve specific risk/return profiles. The result is a redefined relationship between the supply of credit and the demand for it.

During 1996 the notional traded volume of the corporate and sovereign credit derivatives market grew tenfold, from US$5 billion to more than US$50 billion, about two-thirds of the size of the new issuance of other structured notes during the year. Some estimates assess the current notional amount outstanding at approximately US$200 billion only four years after the inception of the market. With the potential to become the least expensive means of financing the assumption or off-loading of credit risk, credit derivative-based structures provide the basis for a more complete market for risk. Although closely related to the interest rate and asset swap markets, the market for credit derivatives is less likely to be commoditised. Even in their simplest forms, credit derivatives are highly structured and tailored to specific end-user needs. Since the causes of credit risk are diverse, credit derivatives are likely to remain highly credit- or name-specific, despite the adherence of credit swap documentation to ISDA conventions. This heterogeneity of credit risk limits the scope for a standardised, generic credit derivative. This may have limited market liquidity in the short run, but it also assures robust spreads for these structured credit instruments.

Credit risk is among the fundamental risks of finance. Credit derivatives have existed for at least 20 years in the form of bond insurance, and in other forms of credit protection constructed from more conventional credit facilities, such as special purpose or standby letters of credit. However, credit derivative instruments are now specifically designed to strip out and trade credit risk, to have a well defined pay-off and hence to be priced efficiently, based on the perceived risk of a specific credit event, such as a default.

In their simplest form, credit derivatives involve an exchange of cashflows between two counterparties, based on some underlying notional amount, typically related to a traditional credit facility. Just like other derivative products, simple credit derivatives can be broadly classified as swaps, options or forwards. More complex structures combine simpler credit derivatives to incorporate the correlation of state-dependent pay-offs. Insurance derivatives, which are closely related to credit derivatives, are tied to discrete events within an insurance portfolio, an index of losses or damage, or some event intensity parameter.

Market risk and credit risk are distinct but inter-related. Market risk represents the variation in market expectations about: future expected returns; the supply of, and demand for, investment capital and investment opportunities; and the term structure (ie, the future expected risk-free rate). In the debt markets the primary focus of market risk is on duration and convexity. However, market risk and credit risk are related, because credit events are often triggered by extreme downward market movements. In other words, credit events are, by their very nature, extreme events (rare probabilistic events). Credit risk represents losses in market value, whether of an asset (a financial claim) or of a portfolio of financial claims, that are correlated with changes in default expectations related to that asset or portfolio. The market value of an asset or portfolio is credit sensitive to EL in credit quality or the asset's migration towards default, much as duration loosely represents the yield sensitivity of a debt instrument to risk-free interest rate volatility. Hence credit risk could be loosely interpreted as the market sensitivity of an asset or bundle of assets to default expectations. Extreme downward market movements often correlate with trading gaps and illiquidity related to defaults. As markets become more volatile, they also become more correlated. This is especially evident when markets are downwardly volatile.

Credit risk is idiosyncratic and heterogeneous, and thus not readily diversified away, because of the contagion of extreme (downward) volatility. Equity or price risk is more easily diversified, because it is homogeneous in its relationship to discount factors and expectations about the residual claims' future cashflows. In addition, credit risk has its own term structure.

In keeping with the modern portfolio theory developed by Harry Markowitz and others, two loans or bonds that are held to maturity have a default correlation much lower than the equity price correlation of their respective firms, given the lower likelihood that two extremely low-probability events will occur simultaneously. Hence the consequence of low default correlation is that the systemic risk in a portfolio of credit instruments is small in relation to the risk contributed by each individual credit. Assuming a low (or zero) correlation with the rest of the portfolio, the lower the relative weight of an individual credit within a portfolio, the smaller its contribution to the risk of that portfolio. Higher correlation results in higher volatility (risk) of the portfolio.

Risk pooling obtains benefits from diversification by optimally combining financial instruments with statistically independent or uncorrelated risks in a portfolio. The objective of pooling these instruments, such as loans or bonds, is to reduce the relative weighting of any single risk exposure with respect to the average return of the portfolio. Risk pooling is the basis of collateralised bond obligations (CBOs), collateralised loan obligations (CLOs) and commercial paper (CP) conduits.

Risk sharing attempts to achieve the benefits of diversification by contractually swapping risk exposures with uncorrelated risks in portfolios or instruments held by other parties. Risk sharing is involved, for example, in derivative product companies (DPCs or swapcos) and certain types of reinsurance (co-insurance).

Risk transfer attempts to immunise the returns of a portfolio or instrument from certain risks by paying a third party for contractually assuming exposure to those risks. Risk transfer includes primary insurance policies, excess of loss reinsurance, financial guarantees, bond insurance, portfolio insurance and hedging with options, forwards or futures. An extension of both the risk sharing and risk transfer concepts is risk spreading, or the transfer of risk across many parties – the fundamental principle of the financial markets.

Traditional credit risk management methods, such as covenants, collateralisation or portfolio diversification, provide only partial protection. Cash market diversification is often not feasible, because of a constrained supply of primitives (non-derivative instruments). Credit risk tends to be lumpy, in that notes and bonds are not sufficiently divisible or there may not be a supply of comparable instruments with the covenants, features, terms or principal amount necessary to provide adequate diversification. With credit swaps, asset managers have been able to rebalance portfolios and diversify away excess concentration of risk with the ability to sell short credit exposures to loans, bonds or insurance portfolios. CLNs permit investors and hedgers to monetise their credit views in a cost-effective way. These vehicles provide access for new investors to otherwise closed markets. They also enable portfolio managers to implement strategies in the credit markets more effectively, on the basis of modern portfolio theory. Risk managers can now construct more efficient portfolios by reducing high portfolio concentrations while retaining the underlying cash market assets and at least some of the returns.

Credit and insurance derivatives could effectively delink pricing from supply and demand. In previously thinly traded or restricted markets these instruments provide solutions to the following optimisation problem: what is the maximum return (cheapest cost of funds) given a particular level of credit risk, or, in the case of insurance derivatives, catastrophe risk?

The flexibility of credit derivative terms and leverage enables investors to run a matched credit book by specifying the terms, seniority and maturity of credit exposures that are not readily available in the cash market. The ability to pay an actuarially fair premium, in order to immunise a portfolio on a contingent basis from a particular credit event, eliminates the need to sell an illiquid asset prematurely in a distressed market. A premature sale might lead to a lower recovery value than holding the asset until full recovery value is achieved.

Since CLNs enable entities to synthesise their own AAA-rated swap counterparties, issuers may capitalise on comparative borrowing advantages. The off-balance-sheet treatment of credit derivatives enables participants restricted to investment-grade investments to gain access to higher returns, while buyers of non-investment-grade assets exchange a fraction of their higher spreads for a lower cost of funds. CLNs and CBO/CLO structures effectively arbitrage the default risk, maturity, liquidity, tax and regulatory premiums existing in the market. One could view the growing trend toward securitisation of credit risk and event risk as intermediation to the nth degree.

There are numerous regulatory and market structure motivations for these innovations in banking, insurance and money management. A more liquid market for CLNs and other credit derivatives can reduce capital requirements by allowing more favourable risk-based capital treatment for banks and insurance companies. By the end of 1997, somewhere between US$10 billion-worth and US$25 billion-worth of CLNs had been issued by banking institutions seeking more efficient capital treatment while retaining loans on their books. These issues provided the capital market with access to 'virtual banks' – highly rated investment vehicles with access to short-term, floating rate, senior priority financial assets.

Through the use of indexing of default events and credit spreads, CLNs and credit swaps can relieve the administrative burden and duplication of capacity in the analysis and processing of underlying credit instruments. CLNs that use credit swaps share similarities with other synthetics that are linked to asset swaps or equity swaps and that allow for tax advantaged structuring – for example to minimise withholding tax or estate tax liabilities.

Credit-linked investment notes as investment vehicles can be classified into two general categories: synthetic instruments, such as CLNs, that share or transfer risk; and pooled instruments, such as CBOs, CLOs or CP conduits. Synthetic structures include both swap-dependent and swap-independent instruments. DPCs or swapcos are special purpose subsidiaries of securities dealers that originate these instruments, warehouse the books (the portfolios of swaps and derivative trades) and serve as stand-alone counterparties for these transactions.

Among pooled instruments, CP conduits are often called 'credit arb vehicles', like the Alpha, Beta and Sigma funds, which are simply CP-funded, hedged portfolios of investment-grade fixed income instruments. The asset distinction between CBOs and CLOs – whether holding bonds or loans – has been blurred, but the distinction between static or cashflow pools and actively traded market value pools remains. Various CBO/CLO structures are also distinguished according to structuring motivations – for example credit arbitrage as against bank balance sheet management. A recurring challenge is to design a capital structure with optimal leverage for a CLN, leverage that will maximise return and minimise risks, in particular credit risk.

The pursuit of lower funding costs and more sophisticated arbitrage strategies requires more active trading and greater trading flexibility. This is leading to a convergence among the sub-markets for CP conduits, CBOs, CLOs and CLNs. Increasingly, the preferred structure is a tranched capital structure for CBO, CLO and CLN vehicles that includes the following elements: CP, repo and securities lending; senior bank revolving and term debt; multiple mezzanine tranches; equity sponsorship; and often credit swaps as well.

These hybrid vehicles match the credit risk and the cashflow volatility of assets and liabilities, as well as their interest rate duration and convexity. These vehicles also attempt to maximise the benefits of diversification by investing in mixed asset classes. The global financial community is witnessing the emergence of stand-alone portfolio structures that synthetically replicate finance and insurance companies, as well as 'virtual banks'. The secular trend toward the intermediation of corporate credit risk increasingly dominates the latter half of the 1990s and has potential to dominate the next decade too. This is analogous to the dominance of securitised mortgages and the intermediation of interest rate and liability management during the 1970s, or the dominance of LBO funds employing leverage and non-recourse financings during the 1980s to intermediate control of corporate assets and restructure corporate balance sheets.

As suggested by Merton, the evolution of legal forms, financial structures and computing technology drives the capital market toward financial intermediation and the production of state-dependent financial products, in order to meet demand driven by the diverse preferences of investors. A revolution in merchant banking and principal investing is re-emerging, with developing corporate finance applications of contingent claims analysis that blend equity and credit derivative-based products.

## The principle of credit arbitrage: relative value in the pricing of credit risk

Credit derivative arbitrage applies the principle of arbitrage between separate or separable markets. As in the interest rate swap market, in which different markets price fixed rate assets and liabilities differently from floating rate assets and liabilities, some credit markets price a given level of expected default risk or event risk differently. Firstly, institutional, tax, regulatory or market frictions often result in distinct and separate clienteles with divergent prices for a given level of risk. Secondly, demand and supply shifts in sub-markets for certain risky assets or for capital result in disparities or anomalies in pricing similar credit risks. Thirdly, divergent default or event expectations in closed or restricted sub-markets can result in pricing disparities.

Ideally, a liquid credit derivatives market could bridge the discrepancies among these markets and ultimately achieve a market equilibrium. When the supply of and demand for risk in these sub-markets become equal, these markets will clear and the markets for credit risk will become complete or 'efficient'. In such an instance, the expectations for default and the prices for a given level of credit risk in different sub-markets should converge, much as the interest rate and currency swap markets have.

Much of the demand for credit derivative strategies has been driven by their ready packaging as structured notes for consumption by the buy side. With a CLN, as with any structured financing that employs a special purpose vehicle or entity (SPV or SPE), the rating agencies' primary concern is the bankruptcy-remoteness of that entity. The rating affects not just the pricing of a CLN, but the breadth and depth of the market for the instrument, and thus, to some extent, its liquidity. The growing institutionalisation of investment capital and competition among managed funds are resulting in an increasing role for reverse inquiry. Reverse inquiry represents an opportunity for investors and trading desks, rather than issuers and bankers, to drive the supply of transactions in the capital market. In keeping with the tenets of Miller-Modigliani, investors can demand, and issuers can supply, securities with pay-offs pre-specified to fit investors' particular risk/return preferences, in this case their credit views.

Credit arbitrage strategies that allow investors and issuers to express credit views include balance sheet restructuring; credit spread arbitrage – inter-temporal credit spread plays similar to yield curve arbitrage for interest rate volatility; and synthetic industry-weighted credit portfolios. Combining equity swaps and credit swaps can replicate synthetic assets (eg, leases, loans, and convertible bonds), or even entire balance sheets, and cost structures. Credit spectrum plays that exploit non-linear credit spreads, often present in the term structure, involve basket trades that employ an index to replicate credit barbells or bullets more cheaply than buying and holding a portfolio of actual loans or bonds. For example, a synthetic credit barbell might involve writing a swap to reference an index of loans or bonds with ratings AA- and B-, weighted to meet a undersupply of BBB- with a given maturity. Credit and equity derivatives can be combined to construct options on synthetic converts, as a play on future credit and equity volatility. Credit-wrapping other synthetic notes can often provide a cost-effective substitute for financial guarantees or fixed income portfolio insurance from a traditional bond insurer.

In principle, a credit swap, the most common credit derivative and the simplest to execute, resembles the financed purchase of a bond. It requires no initial outlay of cash, yet generates a regular stream of income, in the form of the premium or compensation for the assumption of credit exposure. Credit swaps are priced to trade at about the same level as an asset swap on a similar credit. For this reason, dealers compare the relative value of credit swaps against comparable credits in the asset swap market, rather than to the spread over T-bills for a comparable bond. The credit swap dealer begins with the theoretical price for the trade, based on the zero-coupon spread curve for the credit, then checks for liquidity in the underlying asset, which will affect the secondary market price of covering the swap. The premium is determined by the pricing of the underlying credit. The base rate approximates the cost of funds plus the spread. If the dealer cannot find liquidity for the underlying asset at a particular price, then the spread widens until the market clears for the swap or it becomes uneconomical for the swap to be transacted.

One reason why the benchmark for a credit swap is the asset swap market is that a credit swap is an unfunded transaction which requires no initial cash outlay. All derivatives dealers price according to the credit rating of the counterparty in a trade. However, a credit swap dealer, unlike a dealer in asset swaps or interest rate swaps, must also consider the following issues in the market for the underlying asset: the probability of default; the expected recovery or loss; and the market liquidity. Dynamic hedging in the credit derivatives market is not yet feasible. In this sense, credit swaps are treated as if they were hybrids between asset swaps and conventional credit instruments, such as bonds or loans (discussed further below).

The downside risk to a credit swap buyer is a function of the occurrence of default, the use of leverage and the realised recovery rate. One proxy for potential losses is available in the form of published historical default and recovery rates, compiled by the rating agencies and other sources. A distinction must be drawn between default estimation models and credit spread arbitrage models. Credit spread arbitrage models compute credit derivative prices by deriving asset volatility from current market prices in the asset swap market.

Rating agencies, and buyers of corporate securities, mortgage-backed securities and ABS, generally model and measure default risk in terms of the frequency and the probability of default, and the expected loss (EL). The probability of loss can be interpreted as the marginal probability of losing even a single US dollar. This measure of risk represents the risk-aversion profile for an investor who is sensitive to losing any amount. Alternatively, it can be viewed as a risk measure that treats any default as a total loss. In the simplest cases, the frequency of default is similar to the probability of default. EL conditioned upon a given level of default can be determined as follows:

Net EL = gross defaults × (1 − expected recoveries).

Alternatively, EL can be described as the net difference between expected defaults minus expected recoveries.

Derivatives dealers, swapcos and DPCs, portfolio managers of CBOs/CLOs, buyers of mortgage-backed securities or ABS residuals, and risk managers all mainly use different variants of value at risk (VaR). These approaches employ methods such as Monte Carlo simulation in order to forecast and summarise, with a single statistic, the maximum EL over a target horizon and a given confidence interval. A correctly implemented Monte Carlo approach to VaR can capture both the market risk and the credit risk of a portfolio, and can compute both the probability of default and the EL as by-products. In addition, VaR directly calculates portfolio value losses from an asset's migration in credit quality to default, by inferring a transition matrix from historical data.

In breaking down the risk premiums of debt instruments, the difference between systemic market risk and idiosyncratic (ie, asset-specific) price risk can be illustrated in a simpler context using metaphors from the cross-sectional regression analysis of risk factors and event studies of pricing residuals. In market model event studies, abnormal idiosyncratic returns in pricing residuals signal changes in market expectations regarding future cashflows to an asset as a function of new information:

$$r_i = \alpha + \beta(R_m) + \varepsilon_i$$

where:
$r_i$ = return on asset $i$
$\alpha$ = abnormal return
$\beta_i$ = the coefficient of variation
$R_m$ = the return on the market
$\varepsilon_i$ = error term ($E[\varepsilon_i] = 0$)

In the Capital Asset Pricing Model (CAPM) and other equilibrium asset pricing models (variants of the CAPM), excess returns (returns in excess of the risk-free rate) represent idiosyncratic returns not priced by the market:

$$r_j - r_f = \alpha_0 + \beta_j(R_m - r_f) + \varepsilon_j$$

where:
$r_j$ = return on asset $j$
$r_f$ = risk-free rate of interest
$\alpha_0$ = where $\alpha_0 = 0$, o.w. excess returns
$\varepsilon_j$ = error term ($E[\varepsilon_j] = 0$)

The Arbitrage Pricing Theory (APT) and other multi-factor asset models (also variants of the CAPM – for example, Consumption CAPM and Intertemporal CAPM) add other macroeconomic and term structure factors to the market return factor. The APT breaks down the risk on asset returns into (at least) two components: a common (systemic) macroeconomic factor and a firm-specific (idiosyncratic) microeconomic factor. In the APT, the common factor 'F' represents new macroeconomic information and thus has a zero expected value. In the APT model $\varepsilon_k$ represents idiosyncratic risk and also has a zero expected value. This latter risk can be diversified away.

$$r_k = E(r_k) + \beta_k F + \varepsilon_k$$

where:
$r_k$ = return on asset $k$

$E(r_k) =$    expected return on asset $k$
$\beta_k$   =    the sensitivity of $k$ to $F$
$F$   =    innovations in the common factor
$\varepsilon_k$   =    firm-specific risk ($E[\varepsilon_k] = 0$)

The discount factor for the idiosyncratic price risk of any asset, including any debt instrument (as a current value of expected future cashflows), includes the market expectation of credit risk. Credit risk is the product of the probability of default and the market's sensitivity to losses from defaults. Defaults are not directly observable and there is missing data both for debt trading prices and for defaults. Also, debt prices are incomplete due to discontinuous trading, illiquidity and the bid-ask spread. Although noisier, equity prices tend to provide smoother, more observable measures of asset volatility. To determine when a default will be costly (ie, when expected net losses are expected to be significant), credit swaps traders employ tests of 'materiality of default' using prices or the market value of debt. The market value of debt can be derived from the option value of default, based on asset volatility inferred from equity prices. KMV is particularly active in its application of contingent claims analysis to derive default probabilities from firm equity prices and correlations.

Both market value and credit quality correlations for corporate debt can be inferred from equity prices. However, this requires a model that links the asset value of a firm to changes in its credit quality. If we assume that the firm's value is randomly distributed and that its liabilities are constant, the face value of the firm's liabilities acts as the critical threshold level for triggering default when its value approaches this level, much like the exercise price of an option. In this way, the option of default can be modelled as a barrier option. If we treat default risk as a barrier option or a knock-out or knock-in option, both defaults and recoveries are a function of the variability of equity prices (asset volatility, or the variability of expected future cashflow). This inference follows from the notion that the current market value of an asset is equivalent to the present discounted value of expected future cashflows accruing to that asset.

## The role of asset volatility in valuing the option of default

Credit risk can be described as the sensitivity of the market value of an asset or a portfolio to EL on future payments. Default risk can be defined as the realisation of that EL on future payments. The credit risk premium prices the risk of migration to a state of default for a loan or bond and the related deterioration in market value.

A risky bond can be analysed as the combination of a risk-free bond, such as a US T-bill, and a long call (short put) option on some asset (the underlying assets of a firm, in the case of a corporate bond). In pricing the call (put) option embedded in the bond, one can derive the probability of default for that bond. The value of the call (put) option and the implied credit risk premium is a function of the volatility of the underlying asset values. Assuming constant interest rates, these underlying asset values vary with changes in the future cashflows expected to accrue to those assets.

If we model default risk as a barrier option, the volatility of asset values directly predicts the probability of default. The relationship between market risk and credit risk is based on the valuation of the option of default. The Black, Scholes and Merton model provides an option-theoretical approach for using equity prices in order to value a risky debt claim on corporate assets.

According to Merton, the option value of debt is a function of the face amount ($K$) and maturity of the debt ($T$), the risk-free rate of interest ($r$), and the volatility of the equity price ($\sigma$), where $\sigma$ is a measure of the operating risk of the firm:

$$\text{Bond} = VN(-z) + Kr^{-T} \times N(z - \sigma\sqrt{T})$$

where:
$$z = \frac{\log(V/Kr^{-T}) + \frac{1}{2}(\sigma\sqrt{T})}{\sigma\sqrt{T}}$$

In the model of Black, Scholes and Merton, the default premium depends solely on firm leverage, operating risk and debt maturity. Hence the volatility of equity serves as an informative signal on cashflow variability in relation to business risk and financial and operating leverage.

For any portfolio, much of the covariance dominates the variance of any single credit. Covariance is the product of the variances of the assets and the correlation between those assets. The magnitude of the correlation determines the extent to which individual credit variances can offset one another.

## Tranched and pooled structures: collateralised debt obligations

The first CBO was successfully completed in about 1987 and the first CLO was issued by Continental Illinois in 1989. During 1996 more than US$15 billion-worth of CBO/CLO debt was placed on a global basis in the asset-backed market. These securitisations included sovereign debt, corporate bank loans, distressed debt, lease obligations and trade claims. With the growth of the market over the past few years, Fitch IBCA analysts have rated a significant number of these transactions (see Exhibit 6.1).

As stated previously, these securitisations are beginning to include multiple asset classes, such as project financings, distressed debt, preferred stock and private equity. The recent CLN issues that form close substitutes for CLOs are linked to bank loans by using total return credit swaps (see Exhibit 6.2).

In addition to current arbitrage opportunities, driving the demand for these securities have been the appetite of investors for near equity returns with less volatility and bank initiatives to manage economic and regulatory capital more effectively. The primary driver for bank-issued credit derivatives is regulatory arbitrage, as investors

---

### Exhibit 6.1  Fitch-rated CBO and CLO transactions

| CBO | CLO |
|---|---|
| Cypress Tree Investment Partners I, Ltd | Secured Loan Trust 1997, A |
| Ares Leveraged Investment Fund, LP | TCW Leveraged Income Trust, LP |
| Alliance Capital Funding, LLC | Secured Loan Trust 1997, IVA |
| | Big Cap Funding |
| | NationsBank Commercial Loan Master Trust |
| | Secured Loan Trust 1997–93 |
| | Triangle Funding Ltd* |

*CLN.
*Source:* Fitch IBCA, Inc.

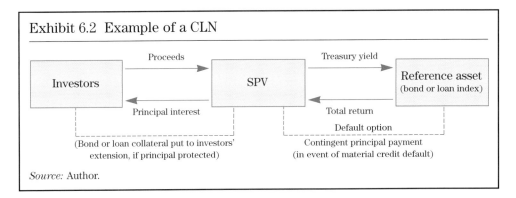

Exhibit 6.2  Example of a CLN

Proceeds → SPV → Treasury yield → Reference asset (bond or loan index)

Investors ← Principal interest

SPV ← Total return ← Reference asset

Default option

(Bond or loan collateral put to investors' extension, if principal protected)

Contingent principal payment (in event of material credit default)

*Source:* Author.

seek to obtain favourable risk-based capital treatment while retaining returns from the transferred assets.

Much like bankruptcy-remoteness, perfected security interest or 'true sale' treatment, rating above the rating of the issuing bank is a matter of legal jurisdiction and of obtaining the appropriate legal opinions. If a bank is to delink a pool of securitised loans from its rating, it must relinquish control of the loans and physically segregate the notes. The bank may still service the credit and remain party to the credit agreement, but it cannot repurchase or redeem the note. The latter also provides the issuing bank with off-balance-sheet GAAP treatment. Loan assignments are easier to delink from a bank's rating than loan participations. Nationsbank was the first bank to achieve a delinked rating on a pool of loan participations, early in 1997. To achieve the delinked rating, this particular transaction also beneficially exploited a technical difference between US federal and state banking jurisdictions. In contrast, CLNs use total return swap technology between the bank and the SPV to achieve delinkage from the bank rating.

Cashflow CBOs and CLOs emphasise expected cashflows generated by the collateral in the pool, in comparison to the principal and interest payments required of the rated certificates. Credit enhancement is provided via subordination – the prioritisation of cashflows. Levels for subordination are assigned by imposing levels of default on the collateral in the pool.

Ratings are based on credit risk, which can be decomposed into three factors: expected defaults, timing of defaults and expected recoveries. These factors are a function of cashflow volatility subject to the constraint of debt service. Fitch IBCA's rating method derives the default probability of the collateral pool based on a stressed default curve for the weighted average rating of the debt securities in the pool (see Exhibit 6.3). The analysis assumes that all pool assets are rateable. Other factors include the timing of the defaults and expected recoveries as a function of asset type. Fitch IBCA analysts also evaluate portfolio diversification.

Market value CBOs set leverage using advance rates or specific over-collateralisation levels assigned to each asset type in the pool. The advance rate limits the amount of debt issued against the asset value of the pool. The asset values are obtained from third-party quotes in the capital markets (marked to market). This form of analysis assumes that collateral assets are readily marketable assets that can be valued, and that market volatility is bounded and predictable.

The primary distinctions between CBOs and CLOs are the assumed recovery values of the underlying assets and their average life. Loans are typically senior priority, floating rate, short- to medium-term and fully amortising financial claims. In contrast to unsecured corporate bonds that, on average, recover about 30 per cent of their value after the issuer files for bankruptcy, bank loans tend to recover 70–90 per cent of their

> **Exhibit 6.3 CBO/CLO rating criteria**
>
> - CBOs and CLOs are structured investment vehicles with similar structural features;
> - CLNs, as structured pools of credits, are also in this category;
> - Bankruptcy-remoteness is the most critical feature of the legal analysis;
> - Rating assignment is a function of expected defaults, timing of defaults and expected recovery rates;
> - The key to the Fitch IBCA cashflow rating methodology is the stress multiples analysis of rating levels along the default probability curve; and
> - The curve correlates rating categories to historical aggregate base probabilities of default for corporate debt.
>
> *Source:* Pridgen and Verna: *CBO/CLO Rating Criteria* Fitch IBCA, 1997.

> **Exhibit 6.4 Investors' appetite for CBOs and CLOs**
>
> CLOs (pool > 25–30 loans) may have a one-class or two-class structure. A one-class structure consists of a senior-rated tranche and an unrated retained residual (equity) tranche. A two-class structure also has a rated mezzanine tranche and a smaller unrated residual (less equity).
>
> Fitch IBCA assesses CLOs on the following criteria:
>
> - the credit quality of underlying loans;
> - the spread between interest earned on the loans and the coupon paid on the securities issued by the CLO;
> - industry and obligor diversification;
> - interest rate and basis risk;
> - the asset manager's track record, reputation and experience; and
> - a cashflow-based default analysis, similar to the CBO rating methodology.
>
> *Source:* Pridgen, Verna and Schoen: *CLOs Meet Investor Appetite for Loans* Fitch IBCA, 1996.

par value. Hence CLOs can support higher leverage or require lower credit enhancement to achieve the same rating, all other factors being equal (see Exhibit 6.4).

Ratings for CLNs address only stated coupon and principal payments and reflect the weakest link in the chain of credit relationships, such as counterparty risk or issuer exposure.

Recent structured note innovations in CBO/CLO structures include:

- equity tranches defeased or principal-protected using zero-coupon Treasury strips for placement in the debt capital market;
- structured debt instruments issued for the debt market by diversified pools of CBO/CLO equity tranches; and
- contingent pay-out mezzanine tranches and trigger structures to increase CBO/CLO leverage further (reducing equity).

## Emerging market collateralised bond obligations: market volatility, duration and the term structure of emerging market credit risk

Emerging market debt behaves more like high-yielding domestic debt than like industrialised countries' sovereign or investment-grade corporate debt. The credit and interest rate sensitivity of a sovereign domicile compounds the local business conditions that influence the credit of corporate emerging market debt. As a risk factor, the default risk of emerging market debt is essentially absent from the bonds of industrialised countries. Dym (1996) addresses this unique feature of sovereign emerging market debt by developing a risk measure that adjusts for duration risk and credit risk.

For sovereign and corporate emerging market debt, duration-adjusted credit risk is distinct from both interest rate sensitivity (or yield volatility of the risk-free rate) and credit sensitivity. Hence the duration-adjusted credit risk of an emerging market sovereign bond – as opposed to its credit sensitivity – can be measured by the following:

$$\text{Credit risk} = \frac{\text{Duration St dev } (\Delta d)}{1 - d}$$

where:
$d$ = the market's assessment of the bond's default probability.

The credit risk of sovereign or corporate emerging market debt is the product of its credit duration (the term structure of the credit risk) and the volatility of its expected default rate (the implied volatility of the risky option). Therefore the bond's total risk reflects its likely price movements in response to changes in interest rates, changes in expected default rates and the interaction of these changes. Therefore the credit risk of emerging market debt is captured by the volatility of the expected default rate and its covariance with the risk-free rate (credit spread variability).

Like domestic high-yielding bonds, corporate emerging market debt returns are better explained by equity factors than by term structure factors. Fitch IBCA's analysis of concentration limits for emerging market CBOs attempts to answer four main questions in this area. Firstly, what are the risk characteristics of sovereign and non-US corporate debt? Secondly, what are the relationships among market risk, credit risk and default risk? Thirdly, what is the relationship between risk (asset volatility) and correlation between industries and between countries? Fourthly, when does industry correlation matter for non-US corporate bonds, and when do regional concentrations matter?

Fitch IBCA examines CBO asset diversification according to credit risk exposure by issuer, region, country and industry. In order to set justifiable concentration limits for global industries, countries and regions, Fitch has researched risk exposure in

---

**Exhibit 6.5  Rating criteria for emerging market CBOs/CLOs**

Fitch IBCA analyses the country's political risk, as well as the underlying economic and business risk of the rated entity:

- EL: stressed default rates;
- diversification: concentration limits by industry, country and region;
- investment restrictions;
- legal considerations;
- hedging;
- credit enhancement; and
- asset manager assessment.

*Source:* Verna and Pridgen *Emerging Market CBO Criteria* Fitch IBCA, 1997.

terms of international volatility and duration measures, as well as sovereign and corporate common risk factors (see Exhibit 6.5). In its research on these risk factors Fitch IBCA performed a thorough review of asset pricing, credit risk modelling and investment literature.[1] Fitch also independently conducted an extensive country correlation study, in which GDP served as the proxy for business conditions (economic growth cycles).

## Swap-dependent structures: insurance derivatives, price-indexed synthetics and credit derivative-linked debt issues

Insurance- and reinsurance-linked derivative securities have emerged as a new asset class for portfolio managers. The cyclical dynamics of reinsurance pricing promise persistent periods of excess returns to the yield-hungry debt market. Insurance derivative securities issued in the debt markets attempt to arbitrage the difference in pricing between comparable credit risk priced in the debt market and 'natural' event risk priced in the reinsurance market.

The categories for capital market approaches to catastrophic reinsurance risk include traditional reinsurance and contingent (bank) financing, as well as capital market securitisations, such as insurance-linked credit swap financing, synthetic reinsurance or third-party event risk swaps. Traditional reinsurance generally involves direct payment from a reinsurer to a ceding insurer if a defined event occurs. Contingent bank financing is a liquidity facility provided to an insurer in exchange for a facility fee and interest paid on the drawn amount.

Credit risk securitisation and insurance-linked credit swap financing involve investment-grade fixed income securities held by an SPV, where the securities may be called by the insurance company in exchange for surplus notes or debt issued by the insurance company.

A synthetic reinsurance issuance – commonly referred as a catastrophe bond or a catastrophe-linked note (CatLN) – is a reinsurance treaty-linked structured note issued by an SPV.

Third-party event risk swaps are structured or 'flow' trades between insurers and a counterparty that involve an exchange of cashflows or securities triggered by a catastrophic event (see Exhibit 6.6).

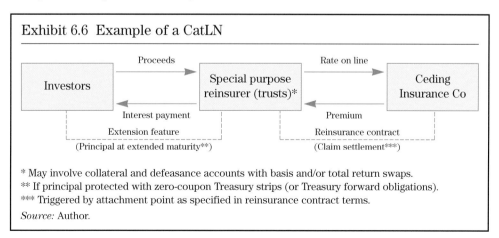

Exhibit 6.6  Example of a CatLN

\* May involve collateral and defeasance accounts with basis and/or total return swaps.
\*\* If principal protected with zero-coupon Treasury strips (or Treasury forward obligations).
\*\*\* Triggered by attachment point as specified in reinsurance contract terms.
*Source:* Author.

---

[1] See Mordecai et al: *Emerging Market CBO Concentration Limits: Volatility, Business Cycle Correlation and the Diversification of Industry, Region and Country Risk* (Fitch IBCA, 1998).

Insurance derivatives are in many ways analogous to credit derivatives – in particular, default options and total return swaps. In fact, default options and credit swaps could be described as simply a form of insurance, similar to bond insurance. Options are used as market event insurance, in other words as hedging and portfolio insurance. Portfolio insurance is identical in principle to stop-loss reinsurance. Forms of principal protection and defeasance (such as guarantees, T-bills or forward obligations) can be referred to as credit insurance. These instruments all serve as substitutes or complements for credit and portfolio insurance supplied by the 'monoline' or specialised financial insurance companies. Insurance treaties as contingent claims are, in essence, derivative instruments.

There are essentially two kinds of reinsurance treaties: facultative and event trigger. A facultative treaty is a proportional reinsurance treaty, in which the reinsurer shares equally in the premiums written and the claims incurred by the primary insurer. In this sense a facultative treaty is like a blanket policy for the primary (ceding) insurer. However, CatLNs are usually structured around an event trigger treaty. Reinsurance treaties are essentially swaps, and credit risk and default swaps employ a modelling approach that is similar to modelling catastrophe risk. The approach, adopted from extreme value theory, plays a particularly important role in the pricing of reinsurance contracts, especially those involving events of low probability but high severity. The primary example is the Catastrophe Excess of Loss Cover per Event (CatXL) reinsurance treaty, which is of the event trigger type. The CatXL treaty corresponds in financial option theory to a bull spread with the market loss ratio as the reference asset.

There has been discussion of linking CatLN structures to oil spills, industrial accidents, satellite risk and a host of other insured risks. However, the rated CatLNs trading in the market at present all reference 'acts of God' or natural disasters, specifically hurricanes or earthquakes. Of the three rated transactions issued in 1997, one was hurricane-related and the other two were earthquake-related.

CatLN structures fall into three broad categories: book of business, index-based and parameter trigger. CatLN investors can experience losses to either principal or interest, depending on the covenants of the bond. The book of business structure securitises a portion of a ceding insurer's policies. The index-based structure attaches to an index of claims as the reference asset. Losses to bondholders in both these structures are triggered by the level of losses from an event above the referenced attachment point. A parameter trigger structure, however, triggers losses to the bond either based on some inferred natural parameter, such as the magnitude and location of an earthquake, or by some other measure more directly related to the damage incurred in a region, such as measured ground motion from an earthquake occurrence. Of the two parameter triggers, the latter, although more complicated, presents fewer estimation problems and therefore provides more reliable model estimates. This would lead to more predictable expected cashflows for a parameter trigger bond.

Rating agencies and sophisticated investors in catastrophic risk assess expected bond performance by first analysing the data used to create a model for estimating long-term odds of occurrence of a catastrophic event. Next they evaluate the model structure and the use of the data to estimate the event risk. The model must adhere to standard practices. Finally, they examine the structure of the bond. Not only must the structure be coherent, but the data must be accurate and complete. All three of these elements must be reasonable and consistent.

The growing interest in catastrophic risk securities is evident from recent accounts in the press. In addition to the Property Claim Services (PCS) contracts already trading on the Chicago Board of Trade (CBOT), rival indices and futures are being introduced on other exchanges. In 1996, the California Earthquake Authority (CEA) withdrew its US$1.5 billion issue when Berkshire Hathaway bought the entire deal directly. Six months after the US$68.5 million fully principal-protected Georgetown Re issue, heavy demand from investors more than doubled the at risk portion of the USAA/Residential Re transaction. During the same period, the Swiss Re Earthquake Fund, an SPV, issued a bond with a trigger that references losses as reported by the CBOT-traded PCS index. A few months later, in a yield-hungry environment, another investment bank managed to place a bond triggered by a 10-year bet on the magnitude and location of an earthquake in or around Tokyo, a region responsible for 6–7 per cent of the world's earthquakes. Security structures with contingent features, such as the Sfr300 million Winterthur interest at risk convertible issue, have also generated interest. Various issuers have announced plans for multi-year, multi-event and index-based securitisations.

These products offer enhanced yields for investors and may provide both diversification opportunities and new capital for insurers. However, the need to assess the risk of this emerging asset class has resulted in a demand for stochastic models that can reliably and accurately represent the risk of loss from a catastrophic event. In fact, according to a recent article in *The Wall Street Journal*, insurance regulators are contemplating increasing their reliance on these models for setting rates. The question on everyone's mind is how the performance of these models is to be evaluated.

## The evaluation of model performance

In the evaluation of stochastic or random event models, the robustness of a model can be described as the insensitivity or persistence of model outputs to changes in model inputs. This is the key feature of any statistical or probability estimation model that determines how well the model estimates perform on average as a best guess or approximation of the future losses from a catastrophic event.

A robust model minimises model risk. Both in theory and in practice we can discuss model risk as having two components: process risk and parameter risk. Process risk is minimised when hypothesised assumptions reasonably represent the true nature of actual events (the underlying process). This dimension of model risk is a function both of the selection of distribution assumptions and the estimation of parameters for those distributions. Parameter risk is minimised as the number of simulated draws from a distribution is increased. If process risk has been minimised – that is, the hypothesised assumptions are reasonably accurate – as the number of iterations become sufficiently large, then the simulation estimates should converge to the long-term behaviour of the actual physical phenomena being modelled as parameter risk is minimised. This defines model robustness: how reliable model estimates are as long-term averages of event occurrences and magnitudes.

An understanding of the following concepts is essential in evaluating a model and presenting its results in the context of rating catastrophic risk securities. The analyst must translate a model simulation of a random event, based on correlations derived from inferences of historical observed events, into an assignment of a rating. In turn, the rating is associated with the risk of loss from the potential realisation of an actual event. It is particularly critical to draw a sharp distinction between probability (odds or likelihood) of an actual event and the observed frequencies from the model simulation.

**Model robustness: minimising process risk**
In addition to inspecting the underlying data for accuracy, consistency and complete-

ness, Fitch IBCA evaluates the underlying technical integrity of the model from the perspective of minimising process risk. Fitch IBCA assesses a random event model on the basis of model structure (design and procedural implementation) and model specification (selection of distribution assumptions and parameter estimation).

In evaluating model structure, Fitch IBCA reviews the mathematical functions used in the model to approximate the interactions among simulated hurricane values. Fitch IBCA compares them with current academic and industry practices, in order to judge if they reasonably and adequately represent event characteristics. Some of these interactions are modelled as probability distributions, while others are functions measured or derived from current research.

The evaluation of the model specification includes an assessment both of the appropriateness of its assumptions about probability distribution and of the estimation methods employed to fit the parameters of those distributions.

### Sensitivity analysis: the key to evaluating model robustness

In order to arrive at a level of comfort regarding process risk, Fitch IBCA evaluates the robustness of model estimates in the following manner: worst case 'what if' scenarios (outlier analysis); back-testing/out of sample tests; and sensitivity analysis using alternative distributions.

Random event models and their resulting loss distribution estimates tend to be sensitive to tail specification (extreme value estimation). Tail specification is a critical factor in the reliability or robustness of the model estimates as long-term averages of loss occurrence.

Fitch IBCA performs a simulation sensitivity analysis of the model to simulations that employ alternative distribution assumptions for both the frequency of event occurrence and the magnitude of event occurrences.

On the basis of these tests and other considerations, a Fitch IBCA analyst may analytically modify the location of the attachment point or the shape of the exceedence curve to reflect bias in the model's estimates of loss (risk), depending on the assessment of the model's robustness or lack of it. In other words, these adjustments are based on the relative sensitivity of the model to modified assumptions.

Credit analysis and derivative pricing are both exercises in variance estimation. Quantifying uncertainty is always challenging, often problematic and sometimes unfeasible. As a general rule, rigorous robustness testing requires an estimate to be modelled as a probability distribution with a smooth, dispersed surface and finite variance. Models that generate point or spiked estimates tend to result in gross understatements of uncertainty – such models are 'infinitely' sensitive to tail observations or outliers. In addition, the distribution modelled must match the actual event process being modelled. These conditions dictate the kinds of parameters that can be used as triggers. Parameter triggers that employ loss-related damage functions are generally superior to parameter triggers that attempt to model predictive estimates of event locations and magnitudes.

Predictive estimates tend to have very large, non-linear confidence bands (ie, very large variance) and usually require a larger sample of reliable data than is feasibly available. In addition, estimation and identification problems for some parameter triggers limit the effectiveness of most model calibration methods. Ironically, model diagnostics tends to be even more important for predictive parameter triggers, especially given common problems with autocorrelation and heteroskedasticity. Furthermore, confounding effects from measurement error in the data employed to specify estimates in the model tend to result in estimation error and model misspecification that, under the circumstances, are extremely difficult, if not impossible, to resolve or rectify.

However, damage-based parameter triggers tend to resolve many of the complications inherent in modelled event occurrence estimates. There are often natural physical relationships approximated by damage functions that limit the effects of uncertainty regarding the model estimate of occurrence. In addition, loss and damage data, which tends to be more readily available and testable, can be used to calibrate the model independently and hence reduce model risk. Since damage parameters are conditioned upon the occurrence of an event, damage-based models employ a distribution of all feasible events for a region, resulting in a smoother, more robust distribution. Finally, knowledge of the structural relationships connected with damage parameters tends to be more reliable and complete than knowledge of the physical processes connected with occurrence parameters.

Other risks inherent in insurance-linked bonds include basis risk, moral hazard and adverse selection.

As with many derivative instruments, insurance-linked securities can exhibit tracking error or basis risk. Depending on the structure of the security, basis risk can be retained by either the issuer (ceding insurer) or the investors. Issuers tend to prefer book of business triggers, because they minimise basis risk for the issuer in relation to changes in the risk profile of future policies or to the aggregate risk profile of an index. However, investors tend to prefer index-based triggers, unless the issuer has the ability to change the profile of the index.

Issuers often like the level of confidentiality afforded to them by index-based triggers, but are averse to the exposure of their portfolio of policies to basis risk from such triggers. Parameter triggers share some of the same difficulties as index-based triggers.

---

### Exhibit 6.7  Mechanics of employing the exceedence curve in the Fitch IBCA analysis

Fitch IBCA focuses its analysis around the attachment point, which is set by the transaction structure. Fitch IBCA uses the points provided by the modelling firm to construct an approximated exceedence curve using linear interpolation. The points on the exceedence curve near the attachment point are employed to compute EL as a weighted average:

- The losses from events of specified magnitude are weighted by the likelihood of occurrence for an event of that magnitude. EL is the product of these two values:

  *Odds of event at loss level and the incremental loss incurred by that event.*

- These weighted values (EL) are then summed.
- The resulting sum of the weighted values above is divided by the total number of loss events (simulated event scenarios contributing to losses). EL severity (expressed as both a US dollar value and a percentage of principal at risk) is the ratio of these two values:

  *EL and the total number of loss events.*

- The cumulative probability of loss (the sum of event increments contributing to each specified loss level) is multiplied by the EL severity (as a percentage of principal at risk). This represents the cumulative EL:

  *Cumulative probability of loss × EL severity.*

- The cumulative EL (summed probable losses to principal) value is compared to corporate bond defaults and recoveries in order to assign a rating.

*Source:* Mordecai et al: *USAA/Residential Re* Fitch IBCA, 1997.

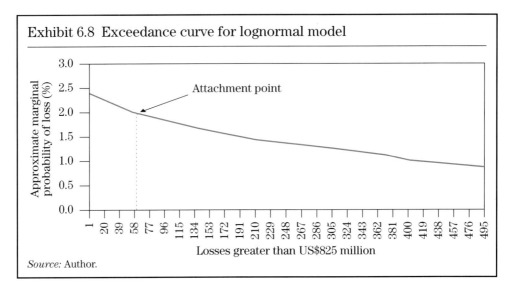

Exhibit 6.8 Exceedance curve for lognormal model

*Source:* Author.

In the absence of adequate risk retention language in the representations and warranties regarding the ceding insurer, all of these bond types are subject to varying degrees of risk shifting, such as moral hazard or adverse selection. Predictive parameter triggers may exhibit the highest basis risk to either issuers or investors, depending on several factors – including the composition of the insurance portfolio, the policy types written by the ceding insurer, the precise trigger mechanism and the degree of model estimation error. The risk retention mechanism is a key feature of the structure of these transactions that is explicitly absent from predictive parameter triggers. Even when loss data is limited, the incentives to shift risk improperly to bondholders may be mitigated with a damage-related trigger, correlated to loss retention-like covenants in a bond.

The rigorous application of these principles to the analysis of random event modelling is central to an accurate and reliable assessment of catastrophic risk transactions. If this emerging asset class is to grow and mature, model robustness is a timely and important issue to consider, not only for rating agencies, but also for regulators, bankers, issuers and investors. (See Exhibits 6.7 and 6.8.)

## Entry: convergence between the credit and reinsurance markets

Recent catastrophic events have resulted in both increased pricing and a funding gap in the reinsurance business. New entry has been stimulated by the demand for new sources of capital to fill that gap. Entry has occurred in the form of new reinsurers and new financial and risk management innovations. Financial and risk management innovations have included an insurance exchange, CBOT options contracts, contingent financing products for insurers and reinsurers, and CatLNs. In addition to the direct placement of CatLNs in the capital markets and investment in CatLNs by CBOs, credit swaps-linked contingent financing and CBO and swapco structures are being explored as primary and secondary financing vehicles for stand-alone reinsurance portfolios. (See Exhibit 6.9.)

A liquid market in these instruments should provide greater capacity and more robust, informationally efficient pricing to the reinsurance market. In addition, deadweight loss or market failure might be eliminated – or at least mitigated. Deadweight loss arises from undersupply to sectors of a market and results from undercapacity and/or opportunistic (inefficient) pricing.

## Exhibit 6.9 Completed catastrophic risk securitisations

| Issuer/ceding company | Amount (US$ billions) | Instrument | SPV | Issue date | Maturity | Rated | Issuance |
|---|---|---|---|---|---|---|---|
| *Credit risk securitisations* | | | | | | | |
| Nationwide Mutual Insurance Co. | 392 | Contingent surplus notes | Nationwide CSN Trust | 2/95 | | | Mutual funds, etc. |
| Arkwright Mutual Insurance Co. | 100 | Contingent surplus notes | Arkwright CSN Trust | 5/96 | | | Mutual funds, etc. |
| *Synthetic reinsurance* | | | | | | | |
| AIG | 10–25 | Event-linked bond | Offshore Reinsurance Co. | 4/96 | | | Single investor |
| USAA (book of business)* | 500 | Event loss-based attachment** | Residential Re Ltd | 6/97 | | X | 144A Private |
| Swiss Re (PCS index-based)* | | Event loss-based attachment** | Swiss Re Earthquake Fund | 7/97 | | X | 144A Private |
| Swiss Re (parametric trigger) | 100 | Magnitude/location trigger** | Parametric Re | 11/97 | | X | 144A Private |
| *Other structures* | | | | | | | |
| Hannover Re | 100 | Portfolio-linked swap | | 11/96 | | | Institutional placement |
| St Paul companies | 68.5 | Loss-linked notes | Georgetown Re | 12/96 | | | Institutional placement |
| RLI Corporation | 50 | Catastrophe-linked equity puts | | 10/96 | | | Centre Re |
| Winterthur | 399 | Convertible dub with interest at risk | | 1/97 | | | Institutional/retail |
| JUA (state catastrophe fund) | 200 | Contingent financing structure | JUA | 5/97 | | | Bank syndicates |
| FWUA (state catastrophe fund) | 400 | Contingent financing structure | FWuA | 8/97 | | | Bank syndicates |
| Lane Financial/Presidio (PX Re) | *** | Equity | INVR I | 12/95 | | | |
| Sedgewick-Lane Financial | 40 | Original discount floating rate note | SLF I | 2/97 | | | |

### Noteworthy transactions announced

| Issuer/ceding company | Amount (US$ billions) | Instrument | SPV | Announce date | Maturity | Rated | Issuance |
|---|---|---|---|---|---|---|---|
| CEA | 1.5 | Withdrawn securitisation | CEA | 1996 | | | Berkshire Hathaway |

* Fitch-rated transactions.
** Multiple-tranche principal at risk.
*** Not available.
*Sources:* Bankers Trust, Sedgewick-Lane Financial and author.

Apart from credit-linked and insurance-linked structured notes, synthetic securities constitute one of the fastest-growing segments of the debt capital markets. In order to distinguish the credit-linked or insurance-linked structured note from other synthetic notes, I refer to all other synthetic notes as repackaged notes. These securitised asset swaps re-engineer the cashflows of existing securities to meet the customised demands of investors in respect of asset liability and risk management. These instruments, issued by bankruptcy-remote trusts, meet the usual standards for structured finance with regard to legal forms, payment conventions and credit considerations. As risk allocation mechanisms, synthetics also resolve the investment market's dual problem of constrained optimisation: return maximisation subject to variance minimisation.

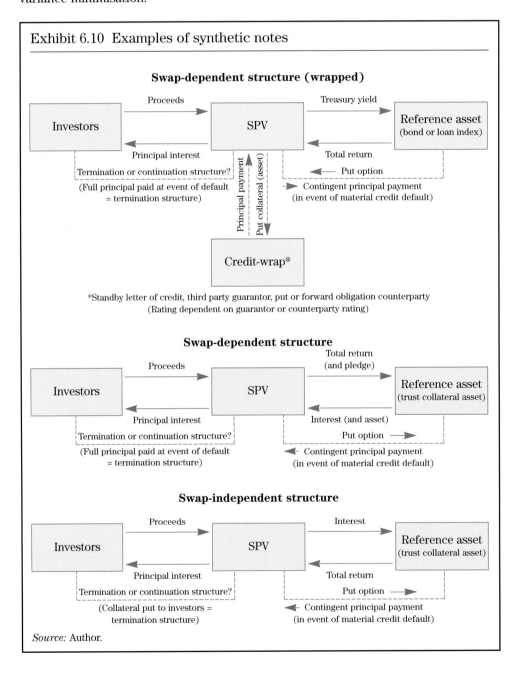

Exhibit 6.10  Examples of synthetic notes

**Swap-dependent structure (wrapped)**

Investors — Proceeds → SPV — Treasury yield → Reference asset (bond or loan index)

Principal interest
Termination or continuation structure?
(Full principal paid at event of default = termination structure)

Principal payment / Put collateral (asset)

Total return
Put option
Contingent principal payment (in event of material credit default)

Credit-wrap*

*Standby letter of credit, third party guarantor, put or forward obligation counterparty
(Rating dependent on guarantor or counterparty rating)

**Swap-dependent structure**

Investors — Proceeds → SPV — Total return (and pledge) → Reference asset (trust collateral asset)

Principal interest
Termination or continuation structure?
(Full principal paid at event of default = termination structure)

Interest (and asset)
Put option
Contingent principal payment (in event of material credit default)

**Swap-independent structure**

Investors — Proceeds → SPV — Interest → Reference asset (trust collateral asset)

Principal interest
Termination or continuation structure?
(Collateral put to investors = termination structure)

Total return
Put option
Contingent principal payment (in event of material credit default)

*Source:* Author.

The repackaged synthetic note bridges the debt market and the structured securities market, while maximising collateral efficiency in order to capitalise on price inefficiencies. For this reason, an alternative name for these instruments might be price-indexed synthetic notes. In mediating between these markets, repackaged notes arbitrage relative value mispricings among: bonds, ABS, equities, commodities and fixed rate versus floating rate obligations. Alternatively, as risk allocation mechanisms, synthetics can reallocate diverse risks from other securities. These risks include interest rate and currency rate risk, reinvestment risk, and call optionality and liquidity, as well as credit risk and event risk. By redistributing or segregating these risks, these synthetic structures create a customised combination of risk for a particular investor clientele, thus maximising the value of the security. They can also result in more efficient pricing for the asset (see Exhibit 6.10).

All synthetic securities fall into four generic structural categories: swap-dependent, asset-dependent, swap-independent or custodial receipt. The legal form of the trust is classified as either a continuation or termination structure.

In swap-dependent structures, the rating relies on both the collateral and the credit of the swap counterparty. The rating will be the weaker of the two credits. Swap-dependent structures are often credit-wrapped, with third-party credit enhancement.

In contrast, swap-independent structures have collateral distribution features, in which a termination event such as default or an unwind results in each party receiving a pro rata share of the collateral. These structures usually take the form of grantor trusts or partnerships, and collateral analysis focuses exclusively on the collateral. In a swap-independent structure, an investor can be made no worse off than outright ownership of the underlying assets. These structures bear many similarities to default swap structures, in which one party pays a spread to put an asset to another. Asset-dependent structures employ (over-)collateralisation (ie, zero-coupon Treasury strips), defeasance, suborbination and/or extension features in order to delink the ratings assigned to notes issued by the trust from the rating of the swap counterparty. Institutional investors with excess off the run credit analysis capacity will conceivably enter the credit-enhanced note market to compete with and potentially displace the traditional monoline insurers. As the credit swap market becomes broader, deeper and more liquid, credit enhancement may become even more commonplace in the synthetics market, especially for non-investment-grade issuers and counterparties.

## The use of credit derivatives to credit-wrap synthetic note structures

Credit derivatives in one form or another have enjoyed a long history in off-balance-sheet and non-recourse structured financing as traditional contingent products. For example:

- back-to-back loans have facilitated cross-border corporate borrowing;
- back-up lines of credit have contributed to the securitisation of corporate credit by supporting CP issuance; and
- other contingent credit issuances have served to guarantee project, equipment and trade financing – for example, standby letters of credit, forward contracts, limited guarantees or defeasance/escrow.

Similar development can be observed in the parallel histories of insurance risk management and commodity price risk management, and in the extension into financial market risk management over the past 25 years. Alternative risk financing techniques, such as self-insurance self-funding, financial reinsurance and captives, now common to the insurance industry, bear close resemblance to the structures now emerging in the synthetics and credit derivatives markets.

Much as synthetic securities maximise collateral efficiency for the purposes of investment and market risk allocation, market-based credit derivatives have the potential to maximise collateral efficiency for credit enhancement purposes in relation to these traditional forms. For example, a total return swap provides off-market economic exposure to the credit risk of the underlying asset for a synthetic financing cost significantly lower than the market rate, especially for a lower-rated buyer of the swap.

As illustrated throughout this chapter, the economics of credit derivatives facilitates their use as substitutes for, or complements to, more traditional credit enhancement approaches. For example, as explained in the section on CLOs, three key differences distinguish a credit swap from a loan assignment:

- ease of off-balance-sheet treatment;
- flexibility of structure and terms; and
- optional use of (implicit) leverage.

In short, credit-wrapped synthetic structures permit arbitrage of all of the following risk-adjusted price relationships:

- default risk and credit sensitivity;
- term structure risk or volatility (duration and convexity);
- the term structure of credit risk (ie, the correlation and integration of credit risk and market risk); and
- more complete contracting through the use of credit (and equity) derivatives to provide securities to the marketplace that more efficiently capture the pay-off distribution of a specific pool of assets, particular industry structures, or the unique investment opportunity set of an individual firm. The potential of merchant banking and corporate finance using fundamental option and portfolio theory applications of credit derivative products is leading to further development of the contingent claims analysis of firm value and default risk.

## Rating credit-linked structured notes

With the rise of tailored investment products, the distinction between investment management and investment banking continues to blur, as buy-side and sell-side firms both participate in the principal investment, proprietary trading and market-making of credit. Credit spread technology and trades quoted off the term structure of credit risk (ie, zero-coupon forward spreads) continue to proliferate. Products in development include:

- Basket options
- Credit spread options
- Correlation products

The key consideration in assigning a rating to a synthetic asset, such as a structured note or CLN, is that the investor should be no worse off than with a comparable direct investment in the reference asset. Typically, in the case of CLNs, the direct investment alternative is an asset swap or a financed purchase of a bond.

Only 2–3 per cent of the OTC structured notes that are issued are rated. So why rate CLNs? One motivation for rating CLNs, and for rating structured notes in general, is distribution to a broader, deeper, more liquid market in which institutions require investments to be rated. Another related reason is to provide exposure to enhanced yields for those institutions that are restricted to investing in rated instruments.

Since the guiding principle for rating derivative-dependent structured notes is credit equivalence, the credit derivative should be structured to minimise tracking error between the credit performance of notes issued and the reference asset(s), subject to the stated objective of the transaction. The underlying asset generally tends to be either a financed purchase of the reference credit instrument (note, bond or loan) or an asset swap involving the reference credit.

In principle, assigning a rating to the structure involves the inference of a default probability or a probability of downgrade for the reference credit. Based on this inference, the secondary consideration is the estimation of EL. From a credit rating perspective, the underlying default probability and EL of the reference asset is the benchmark for designing the default and recovery performance of a CLN. In accounting for sources of tracking error in a CLN or credit derivative structure, issues of basis risk and moral hazard must be addressed. These two notions refer to circumstances or transaction terms that result in significantly greater credit risk accruing to the structure than to the reference asset(s).

Key issues in assessing the appropriate default probability and EL for a CLN include:

- the definition of the credit event(s);
- the materiality of the credit event(s), and the relationship between credit risk and market risk;
- the recovery value – ie, the market value of the reference asset conditioned on the occurrence of a credit event (this determines the redemption value if a credit event were to occur, and hence the EL of the notes being rated);
- the correlation of credit (default) exposures (events) between the reference credit and the counterparty;
- the form of settlement (physical, cash or digital) and settlement risk;
- the discretion of the counterparty in declaring a credit event (especially when the counterparty is also acting as the calculation agent); and
- basis risk and moral hazard.

## Volatility and correlation (uncorrelated credit/default events)

Structured notes, like CLNs and other swap- or derivative-linked securities usually exhibit ratings that are referred to as 'structural ratings'. Ratings generally address the likelihood that a transaction will comply with promised objectives (ie, the timely payment of interest and the ultimate return of principal at the stated maturity of the issue). Structural ratings typically reference the rating of the weakest link in the structure, either that of the reference party/asset or that of the counterparty. In many cases, Fitch IBCA's long-term structural ratings can substitute the higher short-term rating of the counterparty for its lower long-term rating, subject to provisions for the posting of collateral and replacement of counterparty, should the counterparty's short-term rating fall below some critical trigger level. This approach relies on a liquid market for suitable counterparties, and to some extent addresses the compounded probability of downgrade (or ultimate) related to correlated exposures of the counterparty to the reference credit. At the same time, this feature does not unduly constrain counterparties from economically constructing higher-rated transactions.

As with other structured notes, rated (and most unrated) CLNs rely on ISDA master agreements and confirmations for establishing triggers and covenants. Specifying the credit implications of these triggers and covenants for a particular structure involves addressing three fundamental issues related to the pay-off distribution of the credit derivative. The first consideration involves identifying credit events that are related to the payment or rating performance of the reference party or reference asset. Secondly, matters of notification and materiality must be considered – ie, what economically constitutes a credit event and why. The third issue is the likely impact on the note's credit losses of including a particular trigger under the definitions of 'credit events'.

Alternative credit event triggers that are listed in the ISDA documentation include the following types: non-payment; downgrade; moratorium; merger; bankruptcy; exchange; acceleration; distressed restructuring or reorganisation; rescheduling; and renegotiation. The appropriateness of a defined event trigger is a function of the basis risk between the defined event and the stated risk/reward profile of the transaction. In other words, the suitability of an event trigger should be determined by the extent to which that particular trigger matches the potential set of economic events that could materially impact credit losses to the structure.

In assessing credit equivalence,[2] an understanding of the motivation for the transaction is even more critical for rating a CLN than it is for rating other repackaged notes. For example, a CLN that creates credit exposure to a reference credit in a currency other than the currency of issue is a substitute for an asset swap on the reference asset, rather than a substitute for a direct purchase of the asset itself in its currency of issue. This nuance is especially pertinent when addressing risks related to the recovery value of the asset – ie, the EL assessment of the CLN. Basis risk and moral hazard (extent of discretion on the part of the counterparty, especially when the counterparty is also acting as calculation agent).

## Examples of simple credit derivatives, complex strategies and their rating implications

Simple credit option strategies include: selling a covered call; selling a naked put; and hedging with credit puts. A structured note with an embedded covered call can be structured as an SPV collateralised with the reference bond and/or zero-coupon Treasury strips, and the relevant swap agreement.

Selling a covered call is a yield enhancement strategy, where the market risk to the seller is the foregone opportunity cost if the credit spread tightens by more than the amount of the yield enhancement (ie, the premium received from the sale of the call). The credit risk to the seller of a covered call is that the underlying/reference asset defaults or is downgraded, and that the additional yield (call premium) received is not adequate to compensate for the lower recovery value of the asset in its defaulted or downgraded state. In this case, the asset is the net value between the long asset and the short call position. (See Exhibit 6.11.)

A CLN that incorporates a total return swap and assumes the first loss risk (eg, Chase Manhattan's CSLT note) is equivalent to a structured note with a levered short

---

[2] The notion that an investor should be no worse off from a credit perspective than it would be investing directly in the underlying asset.

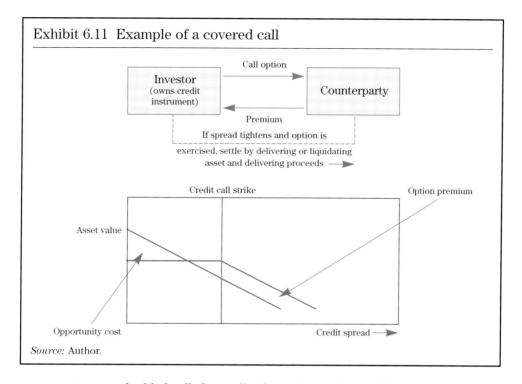

**Exhibit 6.11  Example of a covered call**

*Source:* Author.

exposure to an embedded call. Generally, the rating analysis will break the expected interest coupon down into a contingent component and a nominal, stated interest component. The default and recovery scenarios stress the sensitivity of transaction cashflows to EL against principal and the promised (as opposed to contingent) components of the interest payment. Based on the sensitivity of the various components of the stress scenarios, a structural rating can be assigned to the transaction. That rating addresses the likelihood of credit losses that may accrue to principal and to the nominal stated (promised) interest coupon.

A substitute for credit enhancement through the purchase of a letter of credit or a credit guarantee (a credit wrap) on a long bond position is to hedge the credit position with credit puts. Hedging with credit puts is a way of providing credit protection by purchasing options payable in future periods. Traditionally, similar features have been implicit in many, if not most, repackaged or synthetic notes, especially those note structures where the originator of the structure also serves as the counterparty that guarantees the minimum return to the trust that issues the notes. Whether traditional implicit guarantees are priced as efficiently (ie, competitively) as explicit market-priced credit options by either the investor or the originator of the structure is an empirical question.

The economic objective for a credit put or protection buyer (aside from absolute downside protection) is to obtain a premium per unit of EL that on average is fairly priced. In contrast, the economic objective for a credit put or protection seller is to obtain a surplus premium on average, relative to expected and unexpected losses. A money manager with a credit line for exposure to a specific credit (for which no issuance is available in the cash market) might sell default protection and earn a premium on the under-utilised line, much like a bank receiving a commitment fee for a standby facility. That money manager has synthetically created a position in an asset.

In essence, the counterparty (protection seller) is acting as a guarantee provider by selling an obligation to purchase bonds at a predetermined spread to Treasuries

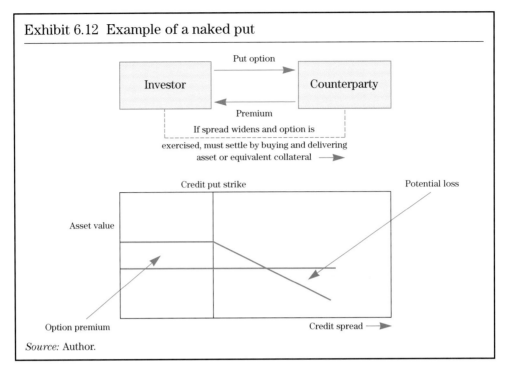

Exhibit 6.12  Example of a naked put

*Source:* Author.

(see Exhibit 6.12). Selling a naked put on a credit event enhances yield and lowers the long-term average funding cost of the portfolio for the put seller. Here, the risk to the put seller is that the credit spread widens such that the loss from the exercised purchase obligation exceeds the yield enhancement (and the funding cost saving to the put seller). Although the probability of a credit event (downgrade or default) remains the same, in the occurrence of a credit event, the recovery value of the reference asset is higher, and hence EL is reduced for the put buyer. The put seller is being paid a premium to provide a floor on the recovery value of the reference asset. The structural rating analysis of a CLN that is long a credit put should stress the counterparty rating (the put seller's rating) as the weakest link in the transaction, since this is the factor that will drive the recovery value of the issued notes.

A credit exchange bond is an example of a CLN linked to a complex credit derivative that allows an investor to earn excess returns relative to a traditional bond with comparable default risk. The investor in a credit exchange bond may achieve an enhanced return without necessarily assuming additional interest rate or call risk. A likely issuer of a credit exchange bond might be an asset manager holding the residual tranche of a CBO. By issuing the bond, the CBO manager is buying first-to-default credit protection by paying a premium to the investor in the credit exchange bond.

A credit exchange bond is a basket trade – ie, an obligation issued by a financial intermediary in which the reference asset is the credit performance of a basket of underlying corporate bonds (see Exhibit 6.13). In addition to an incremental spread paid to the investor during the option period, and a lower additional spread paid after the option period to the maturity of the bond, the investor will be delivered the cheapest of the underlying corporate bonds at option maturity. If all of the bonds in the basket have the same rating and the counterparty is rated higher than the bonds in the reference basket, the structural rating of this transaction ought conceptually to represent the average rating on the basket of bonds. If the ratings of the bonds in the reference basket differed, then a rating would be assigned to the transaction somewhere

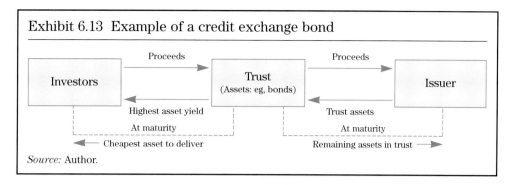

**Exhibit 6.13  Example of a credit exchange bond**

Investors → Proceeds → Trust (Assets: eg, bonds) → Proceeds → Issuer

Highest asset yield
At maturity
Cheapest asset to deliver

Trust assets
At maturity
Remaining assets in trust →

*Source:* Author.

between the weighted average rating of the basket and the lowest rated instrument in the basket.

## Default estimates and the indexing of credit risk

With the growing interest in credit risk management and credit derivatives, there is an increasing demand for credit risk and default indices. Indices of this type have traditionally been constructed as indices of default and prepayment in the commercial and residential mortgage debt markets and the consumer loan and credit card markets. They are now being promoted in a greater variety of forms in the corporate markets. The most common form of index is the total return index, or model portfolio of credit spread performance, which is being promoted primarily by investment banks as a credit derivative trading tool.

This introductory discussion of credit indexing shall attempt to address key considerations in the construction and interpretation of credit event indices. A credit event index can be an index of: loss amounts; aggregate numbers of events (defaults, failure rates); changes in implied credit spreads; or credit (rating) migrations.

Indices of business failures or personal bankruptcies have been published for many years by private organisations like Dun & Bradstreet and by various government agencies such as the US Commerce Department or the Census Bureau. Rating upgrades and downgrades have been tracked for several years by the Nationally Recognized Securities Rating Organizations (NRSROs), and recently transition matrices and default studies by these organisations have proliferated.

Indices of corporate credit events existed previously, but were unsuitable for trading purposes, because of their lack of transparency, measurement error and significant basis risk. These are the very same hurdles that current generations of credit indices must overcome. The hurdles include, but are not limited to, the expense of establishment and upkeep and the maintenance of consistent definitions for credit events.

Although indices can be employed for both exchange-traded instruments and OTC transactions, indices constructed and widely employed by exchanges can more easily be referenced for OTC trades than vice versa. Different models will employ different indices, depending on the objective of the model and its structure and specification. There are three or four general classes of models: forecasting (estimation/ prediction) models; valuation (asset allocation) models; pricing (arbitrage) models; and hedging models (often by-products of pricing models). Different indices can be constructed for valuing, hedging, pricing and trading credit risk, depending on whether the objective is to estimate the number of defaults in an industry, market sector, economy or asset class (ie, the frequency or rate of default); the economic losses associated with defaults (ie, the severity of default); the asset volatilities (ie, implied probability or distance to default) associated with a credit; credit spreads for pricing or inferring default probabilities, total return, etc.

For example, the construction and maintenance of a total return index, which is most like an equity or commodity index, is still subject to far more sample bias, survivorship bias and heteroskedasticity than the construction and maintenance of an equity or commodity index, because of the informational inefficiency in debt prices. Most debt indices employ dealer quotes and interpolated values (matrix pricing) to fill the gaps in traded prices. These information deficiencies further complicate the criteria and procedures involved in tracking benchmarks with minimal tracking error and portfolio rebalancing.

Particularly problematic is the definition of credit events for default or loss indices. Only costly defaults should be included. Credit swap triggers often employ materiality tests to credit events and credit migration. However, it is not feasible to apply these tests to an index of events. Similarly, recovery values are difficult, if not impossible, to observe. In addition, the values associated with credits that have defaulted or been downgraded are often non-synchronous and can either lead or lag the event occurrence.

The first step in constructing a credit spread index is to identify reference assets (ie, benchmark instruments) or, in some cases, reference parties (credit names or counterparties). The second step is to specify for each type of credit instrument the mapping of heterogeneous covenants and default/recovery behaviour into consistent and uniform performance within the index. The potential for basis risk and moral hazard is a key consideration in the construction of an index. Index values will always be subject to broad interpretation.

In assessing the impact of credit risk on the portfolio, our analysis has drawn on principles from portfolio and option theory, asset pricing and interest rate modelling. Our suggestions for estimating defaults have addressed the idiosyncrasy, discontinuity and opaqueness of credit risk. Our introduction to indexing credit risk discusses the use of equity, yield spread and loss indices to define economically meaningful and materially significant credit events, and also describes some of the limitations of these approaches (eg, basis risk, definitional ambiguity, survivor bias and sample bias).

A key to employing these structures and products to manage risk is to consider what motivates these trades – the ability, for example, to strike a balance between yield management and risk management; to replicate and syndicate risk/return profiles not readily available in the underlying markets; and to build complex credit-linked structures from simpler credit derivatives by balancing cost, credit and pricing considerations such as those below:

- the role of the concepts of 'implicit leverage' and 'all in cost' in pricing and structuring a credit-wrap;
- credit spread intermediation;
- default substitution; and
- capital structure arbitrage.

The break-even spread on a risky debt instrument is the calculated yield spread to T-bills at which an investor is indifferent between investing in an instrument with a given level of credit risk or event risk and investing in a risk-free (eg, a T-bill) instrument. Market spreads tend to exceed break-even spreads for reasons related to regulation, risk aversion, liquidity or tax.

As with other derivative instruments, constructing and valuing these structures involves the use of default estimation applications, such as the Stein estimator, and volatility estimation and simulation methodologies, such as Markov Chain Monte Carlo algorithms and stratified sampling techniques. As a rating agency, Fitch IBCA has conducted research incorporating elements of JP Morgan's CreditMetrics and CSFP's Creditrisk+ models into its rating analytics. CreditMetrics employs a VaR approach to default and recovery estimation. In contrast, Creditrisk+ employs an actuarial approach similar to the methodology employed for insurance portfolios.

Asset managers are increasingly focusing on the spread between their weighted average cost of capital – ie, the weighted average coupon of their fixed obligations – and the weighted average price and weighted average maturity of the assets in their portfolio. This has further stimulated the modelling and managing of EL using credit derivatives, the other side of yield management. Bankers and portfolio managers are adopting more sophisticated credit models, based on VaR or actuarial approaches. Similar market pressures are driving credit and bond underwriters to adopt financial and derivative market vehicles to expand capacity and lower cost. Financial guarantee insurers, in underwriting credit risks, are subject to more stringent regulatory and rating agency treatment than other sectors in the insurance industry.

Rating agencies and regulators mandate rigorous underwriting standards and capital requirements for financial guarantee insurers, based on perceived levels of underwriting risk. The result is that credit insurance tends to be a very capital-intensive sector of the insurance industry. Although analysts continue to utilise liability models based on capital resources relative to underwriting exposures, a growing number of analysts are beginning to adopt models with an emphasis on assets in a credit insurer's portfolio, including the value of the assets that comprise unearned premiums. Given the continuing evolution of the credit, insurance and asset swap markets, even rating agencies are being required to price assets in order to derive credit risk and default probabilities. This trend towards arbitrage between credit risk and event risk is expected to persist as the market and statistical risk approaches of the financial and insurance markets continue to converge.

## Bibliography

**Credit derivatives, collateralised debt obligations and credit-linked notes**
W. Robert Allen: 'Integrating Credit and Risk Management', *Journal of Lending and Credit-Risk Management* (Robert Morris Associates, February 1996).

Satyajit Das: *Credit Derivatives: Products, Applications and Pricing* (Wiley, 1997).

David Hart: 'Managing Credit Risk and Market Risk as a Buyer of Credit Derivatives', *Journal of Commercial Lending* (Robert Morris Associates, November 1995).

Richard Irving: 'Credit Derivatives Come Good', *Risk* (December 1995).

Charles Smithson: 'Credit Derivatives', *Risk* (June 1996).

David Mordecai: 'The Use of Credit Derivatives in Credit-Enhanced and Credit-Linked Structured Notes: One Rating Analyst's Perspective', *The Handbook of Credit Derivatives*, edited by Gregg Whittaker, Joyce Frost and Jack Francis (McGraw-Hill, 1998 forthcoming).

David Mordecai and Samantha Kappagoda: 'Emerging Market Credit Derivatives and Default Estimation: Volatility, Business Cycle Correlation and Portfolio Diversification', *Credit Derivatives in Risk Management* (RISK, 1998 forthcoming).

Tracy Pridgen and Mario Verna: *CBO/CLO Rating Criteria* (Fitch IBCA, 1997).

Tracy Pridgen and Mario Verna: *CLOs Investor Appetite for Loans* (Fitch IBCA, 1997).

Mario Verna and Tracy Pridgen: *Emerging Market CBO Criteria* (Fitch IBCA, 1997).

**Models and model risk**
*Credit Suisse Financial Products, Creditrisk+ Technical & Marketing Documents* (CSFP, 1996).

Emanuel Derman: 'Model Risk', *Risk* (May 1996).

JP Morgan: *CreditMetrics Technical & Marketing Documents* (JP Morgan, 1997).

Philippe Jorion: *Value-at-Risk: The New Benchmark for Controlling Derivative Risk* (Irwin, 1997).

**Insurance derivative securitisations and catastrophe-linked notes**
Peter Cardinale and Daniel Moyer: *Structured Finance and Catastrophic Risk* (Fitch IBCA, 1997).

Graciela Chichilnisky: 'Catastrophe Bundles Can Deal With Unknown Risk', *Best's Review* (February 1996).

Graciela Chichilnisky: 'Financial Innovation in Property Catastrophe Reinsurance: The Convergence of Insurance and Capital Markets', *Risk Financing Newsletter* (June 1996).

Graciela Chichilnisky: 'The Future of Global Reinsurance', *Global Reinsurance Special Edition* (1996).

Graciela Chichilnisky: 'Property Cat Woes Have Financial Solutions', *National Underwriter* (September 1997).

Graciela Chichilnisky and Geoffrey Heal: 'Managing Unknown Risks: The Future of Global Reinsurance', *Journal of Portfolio Management* (forthcoming).

David Cummins: 'Risk-Based Premiums for Insurance Guaranty Funds', *Journal of Finance* (vol. 43, 1988).

Neil Doherty and James Garven: 'Price Regulation in Property-Liability Insurance: A Contingent Claims Approach', *Journal of Finance* (vol. 41, 1986).

Paul Embrechts, Kuppelberg and Mikosch: *Modeling Extremal Events* (Springer-Verlag, 1997).

Kenneth Froot, B. Murphy, A. Stern and S. Usher: *The Emerging Asset Class: Insurance Risk* (Guy Carpenter, 1995).

Kenneth Froot and P.J. O'Connell: *On the Pricing of Intermediated Event Risks: Theory and Application to Catastrophe Insurance* (NBER, 1997).

Kenneth Froot and P.J. O'Connell: *The Limited Financing of Catastrophe Risk: An Overview* (NBER, 1997).

Kenneth Froot and P.J. O'Connell: *The Pricing of US Catastrophe Reinsurance* (NBER, 1997).

Sunita Ganapati et al: *Introduction to Catastrophe-Linked Securities* (Lehman Brothers, May 1997).

'The Convergence of Financial and Insurance Markets', *International Risk Management* (EMAP, 1996).

'The Practical Application of Financial Market Tools to Corporate Risk Management', *International Risk Management* (EMAP, 1997).

David Shimko: *The Valuation of Multiple-Claim Insurance Contracts* (USC, 1991).

R. McFall Lamm: *The Catastrophe Reinsurance Market: Gyrations and Innovations Amid Major Structural Transformation* (Bankers Trust, January 1997).

Morton Lane: *The Year of Structuring Furiously* (Sedgewick-Lane Financial, January 1997).

Robert Litzenberger, David Beaglehole and Craig Reynolds: *Assessing Catastrophe-Reinsurance-Linked Securities as a New Asset-Class* (Goldman Sachs, July 1996).

Christopher McGhee: 'Insurance Derivatives: Solving the Catastrophe Problem?', *Viewpoint* (Marsh & McLennan, 1995).

David Mordecai et al: *Residential Reinsurance Limited/United States Automobile Association* (Fitch IBCA, July 1997).

David Mordecai et al: *Swiss Re Earthquake Fund* (Fitch IBCA, February 1998).

Symposium on Catastrophe Modeling: 'A Primer on Catastrophe Modeling', *Journal of Insurance Regulation* (Spring 1997).

**Synthetic and repackaged securities**

Satyajit Das: *Swap & Derivative Financing* (Irwin, 1994).

A. Konishi and R. Dattatreya: *Handbook of Derivative Instruments* (Irwin, 1996).

Scott Peng and Ravi Dattatreya: *The Structured Note Market: The Definitive Guide for Investors, Traders & Issuers* (Probus, 1997).

Charles Smithson: 'Hybrid Securities', *Risk* (April 1996).

**Financial engineering, intermediation, option pricing and portfolio theory**
Harry Markowitz: *Mean-Variance Analysis with Portfolio Choice and Capital Markets* (Blackwell, 1984).

Harry Markowitz: *Portfolio Selection* (Blackwell, 1990).

J.F. Marshall and V.K. Bansall: *Financial Engineering* (NYIF, 1992).

Robert Merton: *Continuous-Time Finance* (Blackwell, 1990).

Israel Nelken: *Exotic Options* (Irwin, 1995).

David Shimko: *Finance in Continuous Time: A Primer* (Kolb, 1992).

The author acknowledges the contribution of previously published research for the selected sections on CBOs and CLOs in this chapter by Tracy Pridgen and Mario Verna of the Loan Products Group at Fitch IBCA, Inc. The author also acknowledges the efforts of Lisa Salvaggio and Jennifer Vento in tracking and reporting Fitch IBCA's rating activity in CBOs, CLOs and CLNs.

# 7

# The regulatory environment

## Paolo Gribaudi
Banca Commerciale Italiana

### The current capital regime

On 11 July 1987 the governors of the G10 central banks agreed to revised proposals put to them by the Basle Committee on Banking Regulations and Supervisory Practices. The document containing these proposals[1] is the reference point for the regulatory treatments applied not only within the G10 countries but across most of the rest of the world as well.

For our purposes, it is important to underline the key points of the current capital regime in order to better understand how credit derivatives will be treated by central banks.

According to the Basle Capital Accord, banks must maintain, on a continuous basis, a standard ratio of capital to risk-weighted assets of 8 per cent (at least half of which must represent the core capital element[2]).

The method used to calculate the risk-weighted ratio is based on different categories of assets and off-balance-sheet exposures, weighted according to broad categories of relative risk.

The basis approach is that OECD government exposures receive no credit risk capital charge; OECD bank and non-OECD government exposures receive a 1.6 per cent (or 20 per cent of 8 per cent) capital charge; mortgage exposures receive a 4 per cent (50 per cent of 8 per cent) capital charge; and other bank and all corporate and other exposures receive an 8 per cent (100 per cent of 8 per cent) capital charge.

In addition, the Accord takes account of a major difference between on-balance-sheet and off-balance-sheet assets (see Exhibits 7.1 and 7.2).

In January 1996, the Committee issued an amendment[3] to the 1988 Basle Capital Accord to the effect that market risk capital requirements should also be considered. This was a very important step towards improving upon the previous approach, and was based on the division between the banking and trading books of an institution. The Market Risk Proposal Amendment was due to be implemented by banks by the end of September 1998. As of that date, banks have been required to measure and

---

[1] *International Convergence of Capital Measurement and Capital Standards*, Committee on Banking Regulations and Supervisory Practices, 1988.
[2] Tier 1(equity and reserves).
[3] *Planned Supplement to the Capital Accord to Incorporate Market Risks*, Committee on Banking Regulations and Supervisory Practices, 1995.

---

**Exhibit 7.1  Risk-weightings by category for on-balance-sheet assets**

---

**0 per cent risk-weighting:**

- cash;
- claims on central governments and central banks denominated in national currency and funded in that currency;
- other claims on OECD central governments and central banks; and
- claims collateralised by cash or by OECD central government securities, and claims guaranteed by OECD central governments.

**Variable (0, 10, 20 or 50 per cent) risk-weightings, at national discretion:**

- claims on domestic public sector entities (excluding central government) and loans guaranteed by such entities.

**20 per cent risk-weighting:**

- claims on multilateral development banks, and claims guaranteed or collateralised by securities issued by such banks;
- claims on banks incorporated in the OECD, and loans guaranteed by OECD-incorporated banks;
- claims on banks incorporated in countries outside the OECD with a residual maturity of up to one year, and loans with a residual maturity of up to one year guaranteed by banks incorporated in countries outside the OECD;
- claims on non-domestic OECD public sector entities (excluding central governments), and loans guaranteed by such entities; and
- cash items in the process of collection.

**50 per cent risk-weighting:**

- loans fully secured by mortgage on residential property that is or will be occupied by the borrower or that is rented.

**100 per cent risk-weighting:**

- claims on the private sector;
- claims on banks incorporated outside the OECD with a residual maturity of over one year;
- claims on central governments outside the OECD (unless denominated in national currency and funded in that currency);
- claims on commercial companies owned by the public sector;
- praises, plant and equipment and other fixed assets;
- real estate and other investments (including non-consolidated investment participations in other companies);
- capital instruments issued by other banks (unless deducted form capital); and
- all other assets.

---

apply capital charges according to their market risks as well as their credit risks (as specified in the 1988 Accord).

Market risk is the risk of losses arising from market price fluctuations for on-balance-sheet and off-balance-sheet positions. Capital charges are applied to items in bank trading books where the banks could include the following:

- positions taken for proprietary purposes in financial instruments that are held for short-term resale;
- positions taken with the purpose of benefiting from movements between their buying and selling prices or from other price or interest rate fluctuations;

---

**Exhibit 7.2  Risk-weightings by category for off-balance-sheet assets\***

**0 per cent risk-weighting:**
- certain commitments (eg, formal standby facilities and credit lines) that have an original maturity of less than one year or that can be cancelled at any time.

**Variable risk-weightings, depending on the maturity and the volatility of the instruments:**
- items related to foreign exchange and interest rates.

**20 per cent risk-weighting:**
- short-term self-liquidating trade-related contingencies (such as documentary credits collateralised by the underlying shipments).

**50 per cent risk-weighting:**
- certain transaction-related contingent items (eg, performance bonds, bid bonds, warranties and standby letters of credit related to a particular transaction);
- note issuance facilities and revolving underwriting facilities; and
- other commitments (eg, formal standby facilities and credit lines) with an original maturity exceeding one year.

**100 per cent risk-weighting:**
- direct substitute – for example, general guarantees of indebtedness (including standby letters of credit serving as financial guarantees for loans and securities) and acceptances (including endorsements with the character of acceptances);
- sale and repurchase agreements and asset sales with recourse, where the credit risk remains with the bank; and
- forward purchases, forward deposits and partly paid shares and securities, which represent commitments with certain drawdown.

---

\*  With the exemption of contingencies related to foreign exchange and interest rates.

---

- positions arising from matched principal brokering and market making; and
- positions taken in order to hedge other trading book transactions.

Therefore, in order to measure market risk, all the positions considered in the trading book should be marked to market. Using internal models, banks must be able to measure the daily value at risk (VaR) of each position in the trading book.

The Committee provides banks with a choice between two methodologies for the calculation of market risk. The first measures risks in a standardised manner (through a 'building-block' approach, whereby specific risk[4] and general risk are calculated separately) using measurements described in detail in the paper. The second allows banks to use internal risk management models subject to the fulfilment of certain conditions. By using internal models, banks can obtain a reduction in the specific risk capital charge.

The Committee has also specified a wider range of add-on categories for which each counterparty must apply a different risk-weighting methodology. The different

---

[4] According to Basle Committee, 'specific risk' includes the risk that an individual debt or equity security moves by more or less than the general market in day-to-day trading (including periods when the whole market is volatile), and 'event risk' is where the price of an individual debt or equity security moves precipitously relative to the general market – for example, on a take-over bid or some other stock event (such events would also include the risk of 'default').

categories are: interest rates, foreign exchange, equities, precious metals and other commodities.

The risk-weighting of the add-on factors for each type of contract is based on the volatility of the underlying derivative products.

## Why the regulatory environment is important for credit derivatives

Like other derivatives products which enable counterparties to manage and transfer a wide range of different risks, credit derivatives allow banks to manage and transfer credit risk.

They constitute a very powerful and flexible tool, and they can be used for a wide range of different purposes, including:

- to improve banks' credit risk management;
- to diversify and strengthen the quality of banks' asset portfolios; and
- to free credit lines, permitting banks to engage in new transactions with their customers without endangering existing relationships.

In addition, the use of credit derivatives is enhancing the liquidity and transparency of the credit risk market, such that the risk management guidelines set out by the Basle Committee and IOSCO in July 1994 seem likely to be met.

In light of the important role that credit derivatives are likely to play in the development of the international financial markets, their favourable (or at least non-discriminatory) treatment for regulatory capital purposes is very significant in terms of their future.

Consistent treatment is also important to ensure that the regulatory regime does not undermine banks' ability to net their credit derivative counterparty exposures with those arising from other derivative transactions. Applying similar counterparty risk capital rules encourages this netting and therefore has strong prudential benefits.

Central banks' current approach to credit derivatives is focused mainly on total return swaps, credit default swaps and credit-linked notes (CLNs).

## The United States: the Federal Reserve System's approach

In August 1996 both the Board of Governors of the Federal Reserve System (Fed)[5] and the Office of Comptroller of the Currency (OCC)[6] in the United States issued prescriptive guidelines for credit derivatives. These guidelines are related to the treatment of credit derivatives in the banking book.

Credit derivatives[7] are off-balance-sheet arrangements that allow the guarantor to assume the credit risk associated with the reference asset without directly purchasing it. Thus the protection seller has an exposure to the credit risk of the reference asset as it would if the asset were on its own balance sheet.

If one assumes that credit derivatives are very similar to guarantees or financial standby letters of credit, then for a bank providing credit protection, the notional

---

[5] *Supervisory Guidance for Credit Derivatives*, the Board of Governors of the Federal Reserve System, 12 August 1996.

[6] *Credit Derivatives – Guidelines for National Banks*, OCC Bulletin OCC 96-42, 12 August 1996.

[7] This definition refers to credit default swaps and total return swaps and does not consider CLNs, which are cash market structured notes and which appear on the balance sheet like any other security.

amount of the derivative should be converted at 100 per cent to determine the equivalent credit amount to be included as risk-weighted assets. This credit exposure will be allocated to the risk category of the reference credit to which the credit default is related (for example, a corporate would be 100 per cent, an OECD bank 20 per cent, etc).

However, the protection buyer may assign the risk category appropriate to the guarantor. For example, if a bank has an exposure with a reference obligation that has a risk-weighting of 100 per cent, with a credit derivative issued by an OECD bank, it could reduce the conversion factor to 20 per cent.

The Fed's guidelines emphasise how important it is that the credit derivative is identical to the underlying asset for which the beneficiary has bought credit protection (ie, it has the same level of seniority; identical events of default and cross default; an identical threshold, etc).

Of significant concern is the maturity of the credit derivative compared with the maturity of the underlying asset. In fact, if the term of the credit derivative is shorter than that of the hedged asset (resulting in a mismatch of maturity), the protection buyer continues to be exposed to the credit risk of the underlying asset when the credit derivative expires. Therefore, according to the Fed, the severity of the underlying asset's classification ought not to be reduced (although the Fed guidelines do not preclude such a hedge from being recognised at all).

Another important issue arises when the reference asset of the credit derivative is different from the debt obligation being hedged (for example, if the reference asset is a bond and the debt obligation is a loan). When this happens, there must be an appropriate proxy for the reference asset, through which a high degree of correlation exists for the loan on which the protection buyer is intending to offset the credit exposure.

With a total return swap, the protection seller also faces exposure to the credit risk of the counterparty ('replacement cost'). Measurement of this should take into consideration add-on factors related to potential future exposure of the credit derivative to market price changes. Counterparty risk is the main risk faced by banks that are acting as dealers and that have fully matched positions.

The Fed's guidelines also refer to credit derivatives that are related to a basket of reference assets, where the protection seller covers losses only on the first assets in the group to default ('first loss' of the portfolio). The protection buyer, which owns all the reference assets included in the basket, may assign the asset in the group with the smallest US dollar value to the risk related to the protection seller. On the other side, the protection seller must assign the contract's notional credit exposure to the highest risk category appropriate to the reference assets included in the basket.

In June 1997 the Fed issued a new paper[8] focusing on how credit derivatives held in the trading book should be treated under the market risk capital requirements. This represents an important step forward in the regulation of credit derivatives.

Credit derivative transactions held in the trading book are exposed to the following three risks:

- counterparty credit risk;[9]

---

[8] *Application of Market Risk Capital Requirements to Credit Derivatives*, the Board of Governors of the Federal Reserve System, 13 June 1997.
[9] According to the Fed, 'counterparty credit risk' is the risk arising from the possibility that the counterparty defaults on amounts owed on a derivative transaction.

- general market risk;[10] and
- specific risk of the underlying reference asset.[11]

The latter is identical to the risk arising from a cash position on a loan or bond. Given the three different risk elements, the Fed considers three different types of position that a banking organisation can take in the trading book:

- matched position;
- offsetting position; and
- open position.

Matched positions exist when long and short positions have identical credit derivative structures (ie, they have the same credit events, thresholds and other relevant contract terms) over identical maturities and reference identical assets.[12]

The Fed considers offsetting positions to exist when long and short credit derivative positions have the same obligor and the same level of seniority in bankruptcy. Also included in this category are positions that would be matched positions, except for the fact that the long and the short credit derivative positions have different maturities, or that one leg is a total return product (equivalent to a cash instrument) and the other is purely a default product.

All positions that are not matched or offsetting are open positions.

Exhibit 7.3[13] describes which of the three risk elements is present in each of the three positions.

Thus with a matched position there is only counterparty credit risk because the nature of the position eliminates general market risk and specific risk. Both offsetting and open positions have all three risk elements, but with an offsetting position, general and specific risk are present to a significantly lesser degree than with an open position.

Counterparty risk is calculated by determining the mark-to-market value of the credit derivative (the replacement cost of the contract) and applying add-on factors that represent the potential future credit exposure. The add-on factors are considered as constituting a specific percentage of the notional amount.

**Exhibit 7.3  Types of risk in trading book positions**

|  | *Counterparty credit risk* | *General market risk* | *Specific risk* |
|---|---|---|---|
| Matched position | Yes | No | No |
| Offsetting position | Yes | Yes (some) | Yes (some) |
| Open position | Yes | Yes | Yes |

---

[10] According to the Fed, 'general market risk' is the risk arising from changes in the reference asset's value due to broad market movements, such as changes in the general level of interest rates.

[11] According to the Fed, 'specific risk' is the risk arising from changes in the reference asset's value due to factors other than broad market movements, including changes in the reference asset's credit risk.

[12] We have to consider that a long position in a bond and a short total return swap of identical maturity is a matched position – but if the short position is a credit default swap, the position is offsetting and not matched.

[13] *Application of Market Risk Capital Requirements to Credit Derivatives*, the Board of Governors of the Federal Reserve System, 13 June 1997.

The Fed has determined that when the reference asset is an investment grade instrument, add-on equity factors must be applied. Add-on commodity factors must be used when the reference asset is below investment grade, or unrated and unsecured.

As of 1 January 1998, general market risk has been measured individually by the banks, which use internal models in order to calculate daily VaR. According to the Fed, general market risk charges for credit derivatives must be calculated using the same procedures as for cash market debt instruments.

Finally, if a banking organisation can demonstrate to the Fed that it is using an internal model to measure the positions and that the measurement is included in its VaR-based capital charge, it can reduce its specific risk capital charge subject to the minimum specific risk charges prescribed in the amendment.[14]

## The United Kingdom: the Bank of England's approach

In November 1996[15] the Bank of England (BoE) issued a consultation paper on the supervisory approach to credit derivatives. Following detailed responses to this paper from various institutions, the BoE amended[16] the capital adequacy treatment in June 1997.

The BoE's guidelines on credit derivatives in the banking book are in some respects similar to the US Fed's directives. For example, if the credit derivative matches the reference obligation, then the risk-weighting of the underlying asset is reduced to that of the protection seller. Also the BoE emphasises the point that as long as the credit default swap is close enough to the underlying asset, it is possible to recognise protection between one bond and another or between a bond and a loan. In such cases banks must demonstrate that there is a high correlation between the two different instruments.

Regarding maturity mismatches, where the credit default swap has a life shorter than the maturity of the underlying asset, the BoE guidelines state that the protection should not be recognised at all. This arises from the correlation between credit derivatives and loan sub-participations, guarantees and securitisations, which the BoE capital requirements recognise as transferring credit risk only where the protection is for the entire life of the underlying credit exposure. However, with total return swaps, asynchronous positions do not preclude the recognition of offset.

In such cases, credit derivatives are considered as being similar to guarantees, and should therefore be converted at a 100 per cent risk-weighting to determine the credit equivalent. The credit exposure is then allocated to the risk category of the reference credit related to the credit derivative.

CLNs are treated in a similar manner to credit default swaps. The main difference is that with CLNs, the protection buyer receives full collateral against the risk of a credit event occurring on the underlying asset. Its exposure to the underlying asset is thus fully removed.

For baskets of assets with different reference credits, the BoE adopts a 'worst case scenario' approach. The protection seller must assume exposure to the highest potential pay-out under the transaction, at the highest risk-weighting under the trans-

---

[14] The amount of capital held to cover specific risk must be equal to at least 50 per cent of the specific risk charge that would result from the standardised calculation.

[15] *Discussion Paper – Developing a Supervisory Approach to Credit Derivatives*, The Bank of England, November 1996.

[16] *Credit Derivatives: Amended Interim Capital Adequacy Treatment*, Bank of England, 5 June 1997.

action. The protection buyer, however, may use the protection only for the reference credit with the lowest risk-weighting, and the amount of protection considered must be limited to the lowest possible pay-out under the transaction.

The BoE's initial approach was to exclude all credit default products from the trading book. However, after banks and trade associations provided clarification regarding methods of credit derivative valuation, the BoE decided in June 1997 to include default products in the trading book, with the exception of those for which the underlying asset is a loan.

The BoE considers credit default swaps to be more like swaps than true options. Therefore, if the maturity of the credit default product is exactly the same as that of the underlying product being hedged (or that of another credit default product in the trading book with the same characteristics), the specific risk[17] of the two positions will be offset. On the other hand, if there is a maturity mismatch, no offsetting of specific risk is permitted. Therefore, if the position is matched, the only risk will be counterparty risk,[18] which has to be determined by calculating the credit equivalent multiplied by the counterparty risk-weighting and applying the add-on equity factors.

The BoE recognises that with total return swaps (which transfer market risk as a whole), each party has exposure to the other as payments may be due in each direction. Therefore, it is possible to break down the total return swap into a notional rate leg (representing the interest payments) and a reference asset leg (representing the synthetic position). The resulting market risk of these positions can be offset under the European Capital Adequacy Directive (CAD) rules. Thus, if the position is considered as being fully hedged, there will be no market risk capital charge (with total return swaps, the maturity of the derivative product need not match that of the reference asset hedged). If the reference asset is slightly different from the total return swap, the two positions should be considered as being offset in terms of the general risk calculation, but there is no reduction in the specific risk capital charge.

As mentioned above, according to the Basle Committee, counterparty risk on credit derivatives is equal to the sum of the replacement cost of the contract – if positive – plus an add-on factor relating to potential future exposure, multiplied by the risk-weighting of the counterparty (in this case the maximum risk-weighting is 50 per cent, rather than 100 per cent). In the event that there is a contract that does not fall into one of the pre-defined categories (interest rates, currencies, equities, precious metals and other commodities), the Committee's guidelines stated that it should be treated as a commodity, thus carrying the highest risk-weighting. The BoE decided, however, that if a total return swap was treated as a commodity, it would produce a rather harsh result – indeed, it would indicate that the bond (the underlying asset of the total return swap) was more volatile than an equity of the same company. Therefore, the BoE conservatively decided in June 1997 to apply add-on equity factors to total return swaps referenced to bonds.

## France: the Commission Bancaire's approach

In June 1997 the Commission Bancaire[19] issued a discussion and research paper to

---

[17] For the definition of specific risk see Footnote 11, above.

[18] For the definition of counterparty risk see Footnote 9, above.

[19] *Commission Bancaire Discussion and Research Papers*, Commission Bancaire, 11 June 1997.

address the main issues for the interim prudential treatment of credit derivatives. In April 1998 it published a new paper[20] containing some amendments and addressing some new issues.

The Commission Bancaire considers credit derivatives to be similar to guarantees given their ability to distribute all or part of the credit risk arising on a third party between the two counterparties of the derivative transaction.

In the banking book, the beneficiary of the credit derivative can transfer the credit risk to the protection seller only if the underlying asset has been offset. If there is a maturity mismatch, there are two possibilities for the protection buyer:

- If the residual life of the underlying asset is lower than, or equal to, one year, the credit derivative must have a maturity the same as, or longer than, that of the reference asset in order for the protection buyer to apply the protection seller's conversion factor.
- If the life of the underlying asset is longer than one year and, at the same time, the life of the credit derivative is equal to, or longer than, one year, the protection buyer can apply the conversion factor of the guarantor. However, in order to take account of potential unhedged future credit risk, the Commission Bancaire applies a 50 per cent supplemental risk capital charge in such cases. Therefore, for example, if the underlying asset has a conversion factor of 100 per cent and the protection seller is a bank with a 20 per cent risk-weighting, the total capital charge will be equal to 70 per cent (ie, 20 per cent plus 50 per cent of 100 per cent).

The Commission Bancaire has also provided guidelines for cases where the asset underlying the credit derivative is different from the asset that the protection buyer would like to hedge (for example, if one is a loan and the other is a bond). In such cases, the protection buyer can apply the protection seller's conversion factor on only 90 per cent of the transaction's notional amount if the assets are expressed in the same currency, or on only 80 per cent of the notional amount if they are expressed in different currencies.

The protection seller should view the credit derivative as a guarantee with a 100 per cent credit conversion factor.

With CLNs, where the purchaser of the note assumes the credit risk, the issuer does not need to consider the risk related to the buyer because the amount received is considered as supplementary collateral on the guarantee. On the other hand, the buyer of the CLN must take into account the exposure to the issuer of the note.

In its first paper, the attitude of the Commission Bancaire towards the trading book was very conservative because it considered the credit derivatives market too small to offer sufficient liquidity to allow a trading position to be unwound with the rapidity appropriate to this type of activity. In the second paper, the central bank underlined that although the current market is still small, it is growing fast. The Commission Bancaire therefore subsequently issued guidelines for the treatment of credit derivatives in the trading book.

In order to include credit derivatives in the trading book, there must be:

- the intention of trading; and
- the potential to price the derivatives and the underlying assets.

---

[20] *Commentaires sur le Ratio de Solvabilité – Traitement Prudentiel des Instruments Dérivés de Crédit*, Bulletin de la Commission Bancaire, 18 April 1998.

Offsetting positions are permitted only where there are identical underlying instruments with the same issue, same maturity, same coupon, etc. This necessarily excludes all offsetting positions between credit derivatives and other underlying instruments or between credit derivatives with different maturities.

Counterparty credit risk is always in place, whether netted or not. According to the Commission Bancaire, add-on equity factors will apply to the protection buyer when the reference asset is eligible, and add-on commodity factors will be used if the reference asset is not eligible.

The protection seller must consider the risk arising from the expected interest payment cashflow. This risk may be thought of as traditional counterparty risk arising from an interest rate product. Add-on equity factors must be applied if the reference asset is not eligible.

The Commission Bancaire has also issued guidelines relating to the treatment of a basket of issuers where the guarantor covers the first loss on a portfolio of underlying credit risks. The central bank's initial approach was extremely conservative; in fact, in order to reflect the leverage risk of default, the risk-weighting should be cumulative. If there are five different credit risks in the basket, the risk-weighting for the transaction should be equal to the sum of the five transactions were they to be distinct. However, in its second paper the Commission Bancaire's approach was less conservative, with a reduction in the capital charge permitted when it is possible to demonstrate a high correlation between the assets in the basket.

The General Secretariat of the Commission Bancaire examines on a case by case basis the prudential treatment of credit derivatives that counterparties wish to use in order to calculate their capital requirements.

## ISDA, LIBA and BBA: reactions to regulators' approaches

The role of ISDA[21], LIBA[22] and BBA[23] and has been very important in the discussions with central banks about how credit derivatives will be treated. They have established a UK Supervisory Group on Credit Derivatives[24] in order to identify the areas where further improvements are necessary in the UK, EU and international regulatory capital frameworks governing credit derivatives.

The organisations issued a series of different papers to central banks[25] asking for a review of the suggested regulatory approaches and obtaining, in some cases, important changes to the original proposals.

The main aspects that have been considered by these associations are summarised below.

---

[21] International Swaps and Derivatives Association.

[22] London Investment Banking Association.

[23] British Bankers' Association.

[24] The major players have been invited to play an active role in the Group.

[25] Papers with the comments on the central banks' guidelines include the following: *Capital Requirement for Credit Derivatives*, ISDA, 12 August 1996; *Developing a Supervisory Approach to Credit Derivatives*, ISDA, 1 February 1997; *Final Version of the LIBA/BBA Submission to the Bank of England*, BBA, 19 February 1997; *Recent Development in the Area of Credit Derivatives*, BBA, 4 July 1997; *Credit Derivatives: Issues for Discussion on Interim Prudential Treatment*, ISDA, 6 October 1997; *Credit Risk and Regulatory Capital*, ISDA, March 1998; *UK Supervisory Group on Credit Derivatives: Summary of Decision*, commentary by ISDA, LIBA and BBA, 17 April 1998.

Firstly, ISDA believes[26] that credit derivatives should be treated consistently with other swaps under the existing capital adequacy framework. ISDA has some concerns regarding the approach of central banks that impose a distinction between credit default products, total return swaps and other derivative products, because of the similarities between credit derivatives and other derivatives – for example, in terms of overall risk profile, risk management and documentation. According to the current supervisory regime, these similarities dominate in all swaps, and related derivatives have been subject to similar capital rules, regardless of the underlying risks.

Central bank restrictions on the treatment of credit derivatives are driven mainly by the following aspects:

- the understanding that there is a new type of risk involved (ie, default risk);
- concerns about the liquidity of credit derivatives; and
- doubts related to the valuation and pricing of credit derivatives.

As regards the first point, ISDA considers that there are many other instruments – for example, different types of bond options (such as simple bond options; down and in bond options; and bond options sold deeply out of the money), asset swaps and various hybrid structures – which have economic effects that are, intrinsically, similar to those of credit default swaps. Considering that these instruments have trading book treatment and are similar to credit default products, it appears illogical not to include credit default products in the trading book and not to treat credit derivatives similarly to other derivative instruments.

ISDA also considers liquidity concerns to be an inappropriate motivation for restrictions on the treatment of credit derivatives. There are many bonds that are frequently illiquid and infrequently traded but are still considered in the trading book, while, at the same time, there are loans which are very liquid but cannot be treated in the trading book.

Finally, ISDA has pointed out that the valuation of credit derivatives is relatively easy using the reference asset of the contract or a comparable instrument of the same reference credit with the same level of seniority. The valuation of the credit derivative is connected to the probability of default by the reference credit and the spread over Libor of the reference asset (or some other reference curve).

ISDA has underlined the similarities that exist between credit derivatives and other derivative instruments. Exhibit 7.4 summarises these similarities, and also demonstrates the contrast between credit derivatives and guarantees.

ISDA wants central banks to acknowledge that it is important to apply a similar approach to credit derivatives as is applied to other derivatives, to encourage prudent credit risk management techniques.

Based on the existing criteria (as mentioned previously, the difference is related to the fact that the instruments are traded and marked-to-market), credit derivatives should be assigned between the trading and banking books. Therefore, ISDA, LIBA and BBA have pointed out the need for the BoE to modify its approach, which does not permit banks to consider in their trading books credit derivatives with loans as their reference assets.

The associations believe that if credit derivatives with loans as their reference assets meet the existing standards for trading book qualification, they must be considered in the trading book, otherwise:

---

[26] *Developing a Supervisory Approach to Credit Derivatives*, ISDA, 1 February 1997.

Exhibit 7.4 Comparison of credit derivatives and other derivative instruments

| | Interest rate swap | Total return swap | Credit default swap | Guarantee |
|---|---|---|---|---|
| Pricing | Market | Market | Market | Private |
| Post-default cost | N/A | None | None | Work out participation |
| Risk management | Yes | Yes | Yes | No |
| ISDA documentation | Yes | Yes | Yes | No |
| Marked to market | Yes | Yes | Yes | No |
| Legal structure | Standardised | Standardised | Standardised | Bespoke |
| Generic risk management use | Yes | Yes | Yes | No (attached to specific obligation) |
| Netting with other derivatives | Yes | Yes | Yes | No |

- prudent risk management practice will be discouraged (because there is no need to mark the position to market and manage it on a portfolio basis with the other trading risk positions); and
- UK markets will suffer from competitive disadvantage (the US approach permits the trading book treatment of credit derivatives with loans as their reference assets).

It is important that central banks should attempt to establish an approach to the treatment of credit derivatives that encourages and facilitates prudent risk management within the constrains of the existing regulatory framework.

In a recent paper issued in April 1998[27] ISDA, LIBA and BBA emphasised, among other things, the need for clear recognition of maturity mismatches and for the better treatment of basket products.

As regards maturity mismatches in the banking book, the associations would welcome a revision of the current banking book rules, because guarantee treatment is not recognised when there is a maturity mismatch. In addition, they consider that in cases of unhedged forward credit exposure (for example, where the life of the underlying asset is not fully covered by the credit default swap), the prevailing risk-weighting should fall by 50 per cent. Therefore if, for example, a loan exposure (100 per cent risk-weighting) is partially hedged, a 50 per cent risk-weighting should be applied. In cases of swap exposure to a corporate as the underlying asset (maximum of 50 per cent risk-weighting), then a 25 per cent risk-weighting should apply to the forward credit exposure charge.

The associations requested greater transparency in the regulatory approach to maturity mismatches in the trading book. In fact, applying a standardised charge, as originally proposed, it is a punitive measure because of the double charge on the underlying position and the credit default swap hedging that position. The associations pointed out the need to rethink the current position and to adopt a more prag-

---

[27] *UK Supervisory Group on Credit Derivatives: Summary of Decision*, commentary by ISDA, LIBA and BBA, 17 April 1998.

matic approach to applying the directives, as credit derivatives were not considered in the drafting of the CAD rules.

As regards the treatment of basket products, the associations consider too punitive the BoE's current approach of allowing the buyer to apply only the protection on the reference credit attracting the lowest risk-weighting, because the buyer should choose the underlying asset regardless of the risk-weighting of the asset held. The associations have adopted a very interesting approach,[28] where they explain that the capital charge is always conservative if the asset with the highest risk-weighting is protected.

Credit derivatives apart, in March 1998[29] ISDA also issued a paper in which it calls on the Basle Committee of Banking Supervision to revise the current approach of the credit risk capital regime, so that the standardised capital rules might be amended and credit hedging encouraged.

---

[28] *UK Supervisory Group on Credit Derivatives: Summary of Decision*, commentary by ISDA, LIBA and BBA, 17 April 1998 (Attachment 1).
[29] *Credit Risk and Regulatory Capital*, ISDA, March 1998.

# 8

# Accounting for credit derivatives: US Generally Accepted Accounting Principles

Todd Runyan
PricewaterhouseCoopers

## Introduction

Accounting standards worldwide continue to evolve in an effort to address the most recent capital markets products. Only with the issuance in June 1998 of Statement of Financial Accounting Standards No. 133 (FAS 133) 'Accounting for Derivative Instruments and Hedging Activities' by the Financial Accounting Standards Board in the United States has any comprehensive, definitive guidance been provided on accounting for derivatives. Other bodies throughout the world responsible for setting accounting standards are at various stages of development in terms of how they address accounting for derivatives, including credit derivatives.

This chapter begins by outlining the accounting practices for credit derivatives in the United States prior to the introduction of FAS 133. Accounting practices in other jurisdictions are generally similar to these, although there tend to be specific requirements that must be applied and therefore consultation with a locally qualified accountant is essential. The implications of FAS 133 for entities reporting under US Generally Accepted Accounting Principles (US GAAP) are addressed at the end of the chapter.

Prior to the release of FAS 133, authoritative guidance on accounting for derivatives is in general incomplete. This is particularly true of newer products, such as credit derivatives, for which even market practice and regulatory standards have yet to fully evolve. Accordingly, in seeking to identify the accounting issues impacting credit derivatives, it is necessary to draw analogies between credit derivatives and other established products that encompass similar economic risks. In addition, the underlying business intent of the transactions must be considered. Based on such an analysis, an accounting treatment can be developed that is consistent with general principles for similar transactions or structures.

## Intent

While specific US GAAP guidance has been limited, prior to the release of FAS 133,

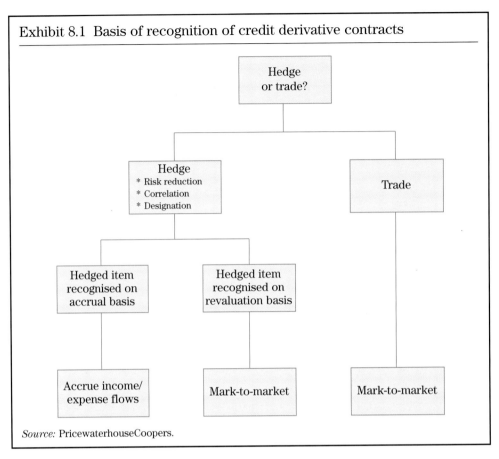

Exhibit 8.1  Basis of recognition of credit derivative contracts

the general guidance is clear that non-hedging derivative contracts should be marked to market and that changes in the fair value should generally be recognised in the profit and loss account as they occur. Where the derivative is considered to be a hedge, and where it meets the risk reduction and correlation criteria set out for hedge transactions and is designated as a hedge by management, hedge accounting may be considered appropriate. In such instances, the gain, loss or cashflow from the derivative should be recorded in the profit and loss account on the same basis as flows arising from the transaction or instrument being hedged.

However, accounting for gains and losses of hedges on securities classified as 'available for sale' or 'trading' (as defined under FAS 115 'Accounting for Certain Investments in Debt and Equity Securities') is treated as consistent with the fair value adjustment on the related security. For example, a credit derivative hedging an 'available for sale' security would be marked to market, with the gain or loss being recognised in equity along with the change in the fair value of the related security.

Exhibit 8.1 demonstrates the above distinctions.

## Credit default products

A credit default product is intended to provide some protection against credit losses associated with a default on a specific reference asset. The product buyer pays a premium to the seller for a future event, such as a rating downgrade or non-performance of the reference asset, which is typically an asset held by the protection buyer. The conditional payment may be an amount fixed at contract inception or an amount

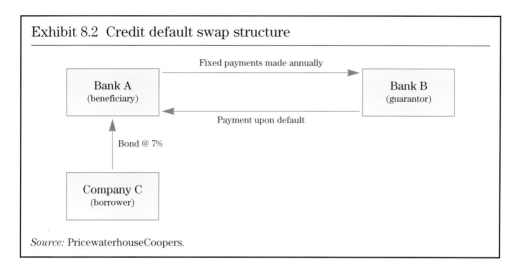

Exhibit 8.2  Credit default swap structure

Fixed payments made annually

Bank A
(beneficiary)

Bank B
(guarantor)

Payment upon default

Bond @ 7%

Company C
(borrower)

*Source:* PricewaterhouseCoopers.

determined at the time of a credit event, usually based on observed depreciation in the market price of the reference asset or of a similar debt of the obligor.

In determining an appropriate accounting basis for a credit default product, we must draw analogies to other products. To help us do this, let us consider the scenario set out in Exhibit 8.2, which shows a credit default swap between Bank A and Bank B, with the bond issued by Company C and held by Bank A as the 'reference asset'. At each payment date, Bank A pays Bank B a fee of a number of basis points on the par value of the reference asset. In return, Bank B agrees to pay Bank A an agreed, market-based, post-default amount or a pre-determined fixed percentage of the value of the reference asset if there is a default. Bank B makes no payment until there is a default, which is defined in the legal agreement.

Let us assume that a bond classified as trading by Bank A and issued by Company C has a principal balance of US$100 million, carries a rate of interest of 7 per cent and matures with a bullet payment at the end of five years.

Let us assume that the terms of the credit default swap between Bank A and Bank B are such that Bank A makes a single annual payment to Bank B of 0.7 per cent of the principal of the bond. These payments are made for the duration of the swap, or until default occurs if that is earlier. In exchange, Bank B agrees to reimburse Bank A the difference between the principal outstanding and the market value of the bond, at the date of default by Company C.

In addition, let us assume that Company C defaults on the bond mid-way through Year 3, and that Bank A sells the bond in Year 4 for US$75 million. Exhibit 8.3 shows the resultant cashflows of the credit default swap.

When credit default products are economically similar to letters of credit or financial guarantee contracts, the accounting treatment can be determined by analogy to such contracts. However, the similarity is not perfect. For instance, unlike letters of credit and guarantees, the pay-out under the credit default product is determined by reference to either the change in value of a reference asset or an agreed percentage of the notional amount, rather than by reference to the actual loss incurred by the buyer. Alternatively, under certain credit default product structures, it can be argued that the cashflow characteristics of the product are similar to those of derivative contracts with optionality. When a credit default product is viewed to be similar to a derivatives contract, mark-to-market accounting is generally applied.

## Exhibit 8.3 Credit default swap cashflows

| Year | Transaction | Market value of the bond | Bank A carrying value of the bond | Movement in Bank A's profit and loss | Movement in Bank B's profit and loss |
|---|---|---|---|---|---|
| 0 | Disbursement to acquire bond | 100 | 100 | | |
| 1 | | 100 | 100 | | |
| | Bond interest received | | | 7 | |
| | Payment to Bank B | | | (0.7) | 0.7 |
| | Receipt from Bank B | | | 0 | |
| 2 | | 98 | 98 | | |
| | Bond interest received | | | 7 | |
| | Payment to Bank B | | | (0.7) | 0.7 |
| | Loss on value of bond | | | (2) | |
| | Receipt from Bank B | | | 0 | |
| 3 | | 70 | 70 | | |
| | Bond interest received | | | 3.5 | |
| | Payment to Bank B | | | (0.7) | 0.7 |
| | Loss on value of bond | | | (28) | |
| | Receipt from Bank B | | | 30 | (30) |
| 4 | | 75 | 75 | | |
| | Bond interest received | | | 0 | |
| | Profit on sale of bond | | | 5 | |
| | Payment to Bank B | | | 0 | |
| | Receipt from Bank B | | | 0 | |
| 5 | Bond interest received | n/a | n/a | n/a | n/a |
| | Bond principal received | | | | |
| | Payment to Bank B | | | | |
| | Receipt from Bank B | | | | |

*Source:* PricewaterhouseCoopers.

However, as with the accounting practice for derivative contracts, the protection buyer may be eligible for hedge accounting. This treatment is appropriate when the protection buyer holds loans or securities, the change in value of which is expected to be highly correlated to changes in the value of the credit default product, and when management has documented its intent to reduce the risk of such loans or securities.

Under hedge accounting for purchased options, the initial or periodic payment for the purchase of protection is recorded as an expense during the period of protection (ie, it is amortised over the period of protection). Assuming that hedge criteria are met, payments received as a result of the occurrence of the credit event on the reference asset are treated consistently with changes in the allowance for loan losses, where the reference asset is a loan, or changes in the value of securities, where the reference asset is a security. As credit derivatives are highly structured products, their behaviour is not always highly correlated to the referenced asset. As a result they do not always qualify for hedge accounting, and are typically accounted for on a mark-to-market basis.

If a credit default product is viewed as a guarantee rather than an option contract, the fee for providing protection is recorded as income by Bank B and as expense by Bank A. Any payment made by the protection seller (ie, Bank B) is recorded as a loss at the time that it is probable that such a payment will be required and can be reasonably estimated. Amounts to be received by Bank A from Bank B are considered contingent gains and are recorded as income only on realisation. This treatment is consistent with the reporting treatment of letters of credit and guarantees under FAS 5 'Accounting for Contingencies'.

## Total return swaps

In general, a total return swap buyer exchanges the economic performance (ie, all due contractual amounts and observed price appreciation) of a reference asset, or index, for a return that typically – but not necessarily always – approximates the protection seller's short-term borrowing costs, plus any observed price depreciation of the reference asset. The observed price differential component may be determined periodically or at contract maturity. Total return swaps can be structured for a notional amount different to that of the reference security, with the exchange of payments adjusted proportionally. During the life of a total return swap, the protection buyer can effectively exchange its credit risk on the reference asset obligor for the credit risk of the protection seller on the contract's notional amount.

The economic characteristics of total return swaps are significantly different from those of credit default products. Total return swaps can be compared to equity swaps, because in terms of cashflows, market appreciation or depreciation is added to the periodic exchange of coupon payments. Accordingly, the accounting treatment of total return swaps can be determined by analogy to the treatment of derivatives. Total return swaps are highly customised instruments, though, and given the lack of standardisation, each transaction should be considered individually.

The accounting treatment applied to a total return swap should follow the economic substance of the transaction. We therefore need to address the principal amounts, and the profit and loss flows.

Exhibit 8.4 shows a total return swap between Bank A and Bank B, with the bond between Bank A and Company C as the reference asset. At each payment date, any depreciation or appreciation in the amortised value of the reference asset is calculated as the difference between the notional principal balance of the reference asset and the dealer price (determined by reference to the average quote from a group of specified dealers). The dealer price will reflect changes in the credit profile of the reference obligor.

As in the example of the credit default product above (see Exhibits 8.2 and 8.3), let us assume that the bond classified as trading by Bank A and issued by Company C has a principal balance of US$100 million, carries a rate of interest of 7 per cent and matures with a bullet payment at the end of five years. The expected cashflows are depicted in Exhibit 8.5.

Let us assume that the terms of the total return swap between Bank A and Bank B are such that Bank A makes a single annual payment to Bank B of all coupon payments received from Company C, plus any increases in the value of the reference asset based on dealer quotes. In exchange, Bank B pays annually to Bank A, Libor plus 1.25 per cent on US$100 million. In addition, Bank B makes a payment to Bank A for any reduction in the secondary market value of the bond.

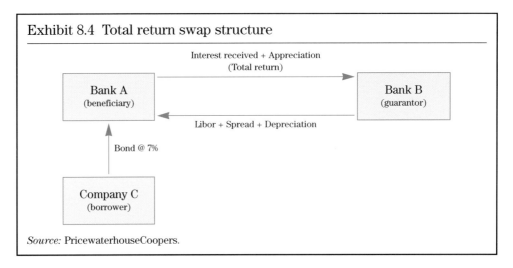

**Exhibit 8.4  Total return swap structure**

Interest received + Appreciation
(Total return)

Bank A
(beneficiary)

Bank B
(guarantor)

Libor + Spread + Depreciation

Bond @ 7%

Company C
(borrower)

*Source:* PricewaterhouseCoopers.

**Exhibit 8.5  Bond cashflows**

| Contractual cash flows on bond (assuming no default) | Bank A (US$ millions) | Company C (US$ millions) |
|---|---|---|
| Year 0 | (100) | 100 |
| Year 1 | 7 | (7) |
| Year 2 | 7 | (7) |
| Year 3 | 7 | (7) |
| Year 4 | 7 | (7) |
| Year 5 | 107 | (107) |

*Source:* PricewaterhouseCoopers.

In addition, let us assume that the creditworthiness of Company C changes in Year 2. Let us suppose that as a result, the secondary market discounts the value of the bond by 20 per cent in that year and by a further 10 per cent in Year 3, and that the final repayment in Year 5 is only US$75 million. Exhibit 8.6 shows the resultant cashflows of the total return swap.

In determining an appropriate accounting basis for total return swaps, as they impact on the principal element of a bond or reference asset, it is necessary to consider cashflows and other factors, such as the fact that market appreciation or depreciation is added to the periodic exchange of coupon payments. In this way, an appropriate accounting treatment can be determined by analogy to the treatment of other derivative contracts displaying similar attributes.

When considering total return swaps, we generally refer to the guidance provided for swaps. Mark-to-market accounting is generally applied and a position in the total return swap is recorded at its fair value, with changes in fair value recorded in income as they occur.

Generally, it is difficult for an entity to meet the requirements for hedge accounting for total return swaps. This is primarily due to the general requirement that the item to be hedged exposes the entity to price (or interest rate) risk. Referenced assets that management intends to hold to maturity, such as an originated loan, will theoretically mature at par, except in the case of default, which would be considered a credit risk. For referenced assets that management does not intend to hold to maturity and

**Exhibit 8.6 Total return swap cashflows**

| Year | Transaction | Libor + 1.25% | Bank A carrying value of the bond | Movement in Bank A's profit and loss | Movement in Bank B's profit and loss |
|------|-------------|---------------|-----------------------------------|--------------------------------------|--------------------------------------|
| 0 | Disbursement to acquire bond | | 100 | | |
| 1 | | 6.25% | 100 | | |
| | Bond interest received | | | 7 | |
| | Payment to Bank B | | | (7) | 7 |
| | Receipt from Bank B | | | 6.25 | (6.25) |
| 2 | | 7.25% | 80 | | |
| | Bond interest received | | | 7 | |
| | Payment to Bank B | | | (7) | 7 |
| | Loss on value of bond | | | (20) | |
| | Receipt from Bank B | | | 27.25 | (27.25) |
| 3 | | 6.25% | 70 | | |
| | Bond interest received | | | 7 | |
| | Payment to Bank B | | | (7) | 7 |
| | Loss on value of bond | | | (10) | |
| | Receipt from Bank B | | | 16.25 | (16.25) |
| 4 | | 5.25% | 70 | | |
| | Bond interest received | | | 7 | |
| | Payment to Bank B | | | (7) | 7 |
| | Receipt from Bank B | | | 5.25 | (5.25) |
| 5 | | 9.25% | 75 | | |
| | Bond interest received | | | 7 | |
| | Payment to Bank B | | | (7) | 7 |
| | Gain in value of bond | | | 5 | |
| | Receipt from Bank B | | | 4.25 | (4.25) |

*Source:* PricewaterhouseCoopers.

that are carried at fair value, it is still difficult to meet the requirements for hedge accounting, due to the fact that changes in the fair value of a reference asset are attributable to a number of factors, including the creditworthiness of the borrower, and it is difficult to determine that any change in fair value is due to a credit event. If an entity does meet the requirements for hedge accounting for a total return swap, periodic interest exchanges resulting from the swap are recorded as interest income adjustments arising from the designated loans or securities. Payments attributed to any actual or expected change in value are treated in the same way as the offsetting change in the value of the designated loans or securities.

## Disclosure

Total return swaps and credit default swaps are generally considered to be financial derivative instruments (for the purposes of GAAP) under the definition included in FAS 119 'Disclosure about Derivative Financial Instruments and Fair Value of

Financial Instruments'. FAS 119 requires that entities that engage in derivative transactions disclose information about their notional amounts, nature and terms. The standard also requires that a distinction be made between contracts that are entered into for trading purposes and those that are entered into for other purposes. If the derivatives are held or issued for purposes other than trading, an entity is required to disclose its objectives for holding or issuing them, the context needed to understand those objectives and its strategies for achieving those objectives, including the class of derivatives used. It is also required to present a description of how each class of derivatives is reported, including the measurement and recognition policies for gains and losses and where these are reported in the financial statements. For those derivatives accounted for as hedges of anticipated transactions, FAS 119 requires a description of the anticipated transaction; a description of the classes of derivatives hedging the transaction; a statement of the deferred hedging gains or losses; and a description of the transactions or other events that will result in the recognition in earnings of gains or losses deferred by hedge accounting.

FAS 105 'Disclosure of Information about Financial Instruments with Off-Balance-Sheet Risk and Financial Instruments with Concentration of Credit Risk', must also be considered when deciding on disclosure requirements for credit derivatives. This standard requires all entities to disclose the following information about financial instruments with off-balance-sheet risks:

- the face, contract or notional principal amount;
- the nature and terms of the instruments, and a discussion of their credit and market risk, cash requirements, and related accounting policies;
- the accounting loss the entity would incur if any party to the financial instrument failed completely to perform according to the terms of the contract and if the collateral or other security (if any) for the amount due proved to be of no value to the entity; and
- the entity's policy for requiring collateral or other security on financial instruments it accepts, and a description of the collateral on instruments currently held.

The Securities and Exchange Commission (SEC) has issued new market risk disclosure requirements, which SEC registrants must include in all filings that cover audited financial statements for fiscal years ended after 15 June 1998. In particular, the new rules will require:

- descriptions of the accounting policies used to account for financial and commodity derivative instruments, the types of derivatives accounted for under each method (together with the criteria for inclusion under each method) and where and when derivative gains or losses are reported in the financial statements;
- disclosure, outside the financial statements, of quantitative information on market risk for derivative and other financial instruments (the rules allow the presentation of this information by means of: a table of fair values and contract terms sufficient to determine the future cashflows from these instruments; sensitivity analysis results expressing hypothetical losses due to hypothetical changes in market rates; or Value-at-Risk disclosures expressing potential losses that might arise from adverse market movements, given a selected likelihood of occurrence over a selected time interval); and
- disclosure of qualitative market risk for derivative and other financial instruments, including the nature of primary market exposures at the period end, a narrative

description of the strategy for managing exposures and a description of the material changes in primary exposures and how these were managed.

## Accounting developments

As noted in the introduction to this chapter, FAS 133 must be applied for all fiscal quarters of all fiscal years beginning after 15 June 1999. FAS 133 standardises accounting for derivative instruments by requiring that all derivatives be reported on the balance sheet at fair value regardless of any hedging relationship that may exist. The corresponding derivative gains and losses can then be reported based on the hedge relationship that exists, if any. FAS 133 describes three primary types of hedge relationships: fair value hedge, cashflow hedge and foreign currency hedge.

### Fair value hedge

A fair value hedge is a hedge of the exposure to changes in the fair value, either of a recognised asset or liability or of a firm commitment, that are attributable to particular types of risks. FAS 133 limits the types of risks inherent in financial assets and liabilities that can be hedged to price changes of: the entire hedged item; interest rate risk; credit risk; and foreign currency risk.

*Accounting for fair value hedges*

For fair value hedges, change in the fair value of the hedging derivative is reported as an asset or liability on the balance sheet, with changes in its value reported in earnings. Change in the fair value of the designated asset or liability attributable to the hedged risk adjusts the basis of the hedged asset or liability, with the offsetting amount also reported in earnings. For a hedge of an available for sale (AFS) security, the change in fair value of the AFS security attributable to the hedged risk is recorded in earnings, as opposed to in the separate FAS 115 component of equity. Under FAS 133, any ineffectiveness or imperfection in the hedge impacts earnings. Under previous hedge accounting rules, if the hedging relationship qualified for hedge accounting, hedge ineffectiveness was generally not immediately recognised in earnings.

### Cashflow hedges

A cashflow hedge is a hedge of the exposure to variability in the cashflows, either of a recognised asset or liability or of a forecast transaction, that is attributable to particular types of risks (for a list of these risks, see the section 'Fair value hedge', above).

*Accounting for cashflow hedges*

For cashflow hedges, change in the fair value of the hedging derivative is reported on the balance sheet as an asset or liability. The corresponding derivative gains or losses, which represent the effective portion of the hedge, are initially recognised in other comprehensive income (ie, as equity, not earnings) and subsequently recognised or amortised to earnings concurrently with the earnings recognition pattern of the hedged item.

In order to qualify for one of the hedge categories, an entity must have formal documentation of the hedging instrument(s) and the hedged item(s) at the inception of the hedge and on an ongoing basis. This documentation should specify the hedging instrument, the hedged item and the nature of the risk being hedged. It must also describe a reasonable basis for how the entity plans to assess the effectiveness of the hedging instrument. An assessment of the effectiveness of the hedge must be made on at least a quarterly basis, and the hedge must be highly effective at inception and on an ongoing basis.

### Exclusion of certain credit derivatives

Certain credit derivatives that have the characteristics of financial guarantees are excluded from the scope of FAS 133. Specifically, FAS 133 will exclude an insurance contract 'if it entitles the holder to be compensated only if, as a result of an identifiable insurable event, the holder incurs a liability or there is an adverse change in the value of a specific asset or liability for which the holder is at risk'. Credit derivatives under which reimbursement is made to the guaranteed party for a loss incurred because the debtor fails to pay when payment is due (ie, an identifiable insurable event) are considered guarantees and are therefore excluded from the requirements of FAS 133. However, financial guarantee contracts are subject to the requirements of FAS 133 if they provide for payment to be made in response simply to changes in an underlying (eg, a reduction in the debtor's creditworthiness). All other credit derivatives must be accounted for under this new standard. One example of a credit derivative contract that is not exempt from FAS 133 is a credit-indexed contract that requires a payment to be made due to changes in the creditworthiness of a specified entity, even if neither party incurs a loss due to the change (other than the loss caused by the payment under the credit-indexed contract).

### Disclosure

For credit derivatives that are considered to be derivatives and subject to the requirements of FAS 133, an entity is required to disclose its objectives for holding or issuing such instruments, the context needed to understand those objectives and its strategies for achieving those objectives. The disclosure should distinguish between fair value hedges, cashflow hedges and all other types of credit derivatives. It should also include a summary of the risk management policy for each of type of hedge, including a description of the transactions for which risks are hedged.

For those instruments not designated as hedging instruments, the purpose of the credit derivative activity should be described. Additional quantitative disclosure is required for credit derivatives that have been designated as fair value or cashflow hedging instruments.

# 9

# Euro cash and euro futures markets: a look into the next millennium

Dr Jochen Schober and Dr Olaf Liedtke
Helaba Economics Department

The European financial markets are poised to enter a new age. The single currency will overcome the fragmentation of the national capital markets that still exist and European cash and futures markets will swiftly develop. In the process, the euro will intensify the consolidation already taking place on the more than 20 European derivatives exchanges, while the euro capital markets for equities and, above all, for bonds will gain considerably in breadth and depth as a result of EMU.

This applies in particular to the cash and futures markets on which, even today, financial market products with largely uniform market conventions and techniques are traded across borders. In this respect, the euro will prove to be a catalyst: it will enhance transparency, promote competition and bring additional liquidity into the market. As a result, both capital and risk allocation will be improved – on the cash market investors will have a broader spectrum of investment instruments at their disposal with a generous spread of risk/return alternatives, and on the futures markets the efficiency of instruments for hedging price risks will increase appreciably owing to increased liquidity.

Admittedly, inside the single currency area considerations of risk will concentrate on the creditworthiness of borrowers and issuers, thus leading to a premium on the yields of the benchmark bond. In Europe, credit risk, which, with the introduction of the euro, will become of greater interest to investors than hitherto, may well intensify the use of the new derivative instruments – credit derivatives – with which changes in credit risk can be hedged.

This chapter will examine the general impact that the single currency is expected to have on Europe's financial markets, before assessing its effect on the use of credit derivatives and on the future prospects of the markets in general.

## The equity markets

In comparison with the United States, continental Europe's equity markets are underdeveloped and severely fragmented. At present, trading in risk-bearing securities in the EU is spread over 32 less liquid and, in part, low-capitalised markets. Whereas equity market capitalisation – in terms of the relationship between the market value of the capital stock and the GDP of the country in question – averages 44 per cent among the 'euro 11', in the United States it is around 130 per cent. Front-runner among the euro 11, thanks to the fantastic pace of its economic progress, is the Irish equity market, with a capitalisation of 65 per cent of GDP. Germany's relative place, with shares in circulation accounting for just under 40 per cent, is in the middle of the European field. Today, the future euro area accounts for a total of about 15 per cent of the world's stock market. Thus it is still roughly 10 per cent less than the yen equity market. Uncontested market leaders are US stocks, which dominate with 50 per cent of the world equity market.

A unified European equity market will, however, only develop gradually, in step with the harmonisation of the various national stock exchange laws, accounting standards and tax systems to European norms. All the same, the European equity market will profit significantly from the introduction of the single currency. Thanks to the elimination of the foreign currency risk within the euro area, institutional investors, especially insurance companies, will in future be able to orient their portfolios more strongly towards the single European market. The necessity, with regard to premium income and pay-outs, of ensuring that currencies are matched will by definition be fulfilled in a number of countries.

Two further factors strongly suggest that the equity culture in Europe will gain impetus. One is the consequence of demographic trends in Europe, which will cause the provision of private pension schemes to expand. Experience shows that, taking inflation and taxes into account, shares offer high yields – thus an increasing proportion of these private savings will be invested in top-quality securities. The second factor is that the euro will make it easier to compare the relative earnings strength of individual European capital markets, so that competition in the investment fund industry will be keener. This pressure for performance is likely to promote demand for risk-bearing securities of innovative and strong-growth companies, and will mean further impetus for the stock market.

## The eurobond market

After the introduction of the single currency, the eurobond market, even without the UK bond markets, will occupy second place in the world league, after the US market but well ahead of Japan's. As currency considerations concerning individual borrowers will no longer play a role in the single currency area, investment decisions will be able to concentrate on a larger number of issuers and a greater range of credit risks. This will enhance the appeal of the eurobond market, particularly for institutional investors. The bond markets in the euro 11 will quickly tend towards convergence due to the redenomination of outstanding public-sector and large-volume private bond issues, especially as new public-sector bonds, in line with the EU Treaty, must be denominated in the new currency as of 1 January 1999.

## The futures markets

At present there are 16 futures markets operating in the euro area. Trading in futures and options contracts on interest rate paper dominates business in index derivatives of shares and bonds. In 1997, turnover in futures transactions rose by US$15 billion to US$100 billion. This corresponds to a traded volume of 161.3 million contracts on the euro futures markets. In terms of interest rate futures within the euro area, the

Deutsche Termin Börse (DTB) held the lead in 1997 with a market share of 42 per cent, followed by Matif, which took second place with roughly 35 per cent. On the other derivatives exchanges, business in interest rate futures was of subordinate importance.

In Europe, London continues to hold first place in interest rate derivatives trading. On the London International Financial Futures and Options Exchange (Liffe), just under 170 million contracts were traded in 1997. In options business, the DTB and the Netherlands futures exchange have a clear lead over the other European derivatives exchanges. Nevertheless, these turnover figures cannot be extrapolated into the future for the futures exchanges of the euro 11. The host of existing hedging instruments for government bonds in the variously denominated currencies expresses the diverging interest rate trends in the various national currency areas. With the disappearance of foreign currency risks within the euro area, the number of interest rate derivatives contracts required will fall considerably. Bond yields of the various national states within the euro area will largely run parallel, thanks to the unified monetary policy and the gradual convergence of business cycles. Those interest rate differences still persisting between bonds with the same features in the euro area will be determined exclusively by the creditworthiness of the issuers. They will reflect the credit risk discounted in the yields.

It is likely that most trading in interest rate futures products will become superfluous when EMU begins. As a result of the unified monetary policy, money market futures still denominated in various currencies will be replaced by futures contracts in, for example, euribor – the future euro money market interest rate. A one-month and a three-month euro money market future may well suffice to cover hedging requirements in euro money market dealings. A lively trade in interest rate futures products presupposes, of course, that the euro spot market achieves the required market depth to enable European market-makers to carry out their money dealings at the rates they quote on both the sell and the buy sides. Inadequate liquidity in the spot market, with diverging buy and sell prices, will reduce the quality of hedging instruments, and market participants may then seek alternative market segments, perhaps even offshore centres.

## The role of a euro benchmark bond

According to proposals of the Bank for International Settlements (BIS), in the approaching 'age of the euro' a broad range of fixed income paper should be deliverable in order to fulfil futures contracts on bond market securities. A fictitious euro benchmark bond as a basis instrument would underlie all interest rate futures and physical delivery would be possible. Market participants could, in the case of final delivery, use bonds with corresponding maturities issued by any of the euro area central governments. Given a completely integrated and homogenous market for bonds issued by euro area central governments, this construction would broaden liquidity through the optimal linkage of the cash and futures markets. Similar to the United States, where several liquid contracts for US Treasuries are quoted at the Chicago Board of Trade, complete coverage of the yield curve for the public-sector bonds of euro area central governments would be ensured through a group of futures contracts.

## The drawbacks of basket contracts

However, compared with the United States, where the paper of only one borrower – that of the federal government – is available for delivery, in the case of the fictitious euro area central government bond, all the bonds of the central governments in the euro area could be delivered at contract maturity. For market players, this contract specification would afford a degree of freedom. The counterparties could deliver the paper that for them is the 'cheapest to deliver'; ie, they could choose the bond that contains the highest credit risk. Thus, for example, market players have always used Italian government bonds when delivering on an Ecu bond futures contract introduced by Liffe in 1991. Because of the lower creditworthiness, Ecu-denominated Italian bonds carried higher yields than British or French Ecu paper. If systemic yield differentials exist, this contract mutates from a *de jure* basket future into a *de facto* future on the least creditworthy borrower.

In 1992 Liffe found, with the future on the Ecu bond, that Gresham's law (according to which bad money drives out good money) makes acceptance of a contract by a market player more difficult and can lead to the discontinuance of trading. Due to the high volatility of the Ecu rates for Italian securities – and also therefore the high volatility of the interest rate spread of other paper to be delivered – the Ecu future was not able to fulfil adequately its hedging function for Ecu bond portfolios, so that market liquidity and also the hedge efficiency of the contract deteriorated accordingly. In the end, steadily declining turnover forced Liffe to withdraw the Ecu bond future from the market after only a year.

## Creditworthiness and interest rate spreads

Admittedly, an open question at present is whether the volatility of interest rate spreads will substantially change when the euro is completely in place. The spreads express lenders' varying appraisals of creditworthiness and these are determined in the first instance by the expected soundness of public-sector finances. Ratings of the creditworthiness of public-sector borrowers, however, are hardly likely to be influenced by high volatility, as expectations of national inflation are already priced in the yields and as the rating agencies have awarded public-sector borrowers in the euro area a first-class seal of approval. True, the agencies will continue to monitor and evaluate for rating purposes any further retrenchment measures taken by central governments. Nonetheless, creditworthiness ratings will probably be of longer duration so that we can expect very stable and narrow yield spreads in the euro area. A divergence of interest rate differentials within the euro area is of course conceivable during any periods of political crisis that may occur in the process of unification, but this is likely to be only a temporary phenomenon. It cannot be ruled out, though, that a basket future comprising individual futures exchanges will be tested to see if the spread development in the single currency union has proved sufficiently stable. In this case, conversion factors could be applied which would standardise the bonds of various borrowers and overcome the distortion created by the 'cheapest to deliver' problem. In particular, the derivatives exchanges, which continue to rely on the advantages of floor trading, could promptly offer these product innovations.

### The role of credit derivatives

The increased focus on credit risk that is expected to result from the introduction of the euro will enhance the profile and the use of credit derivatives. Nevertheless, the growth of this market segment is only dependent to a limited extent on the introduction of the single currency.

First, credit derivatives do not represent standardised contracts, but are individually designed agreements between two market participants. They belong to the class of over-the-counter (OTC) derivatives, for which liquidity considerations are of minor significance.

Secondly, in Europe, the market for industrial bonds raising corporate funds is of subordinate importance, so that credit derivatives can hardly exercise an arbitrage function between the bond and credit markets. Moreover, it remains an open question as to whether in view of the close interlinking of the corporate and banking sectors in Europe a liquid market for corporate bonds can be developed.

A third factor is that Europe's universal banking system gives banks the chance to adjust their loan portfolios optimally to their risk propensities.

Finally, as an alternative to credit derivatives, the sale of claims to issuing houses makes it possible to place these credits on the bond market in the form of asset-backed securities. This procedure has the advantage that banks' own capital resources are freed up, whereas the use of credit derivatives must be backed by the use of own capital, and thus from the yield aspect constitutes the more cost-intensive way of reducing credit risk.

## Trading systems and new products

Floor trading, the so-called 'open outcry', in contrast to electronic trading, allows the implementation of new products, without long waiting periods and without high investment costs for the trading system. Should such a contract turn out to be a flop, it can be deleted from the product range without great losses for the exchange. In addition, there is the fact that newly introduced contracts enjoy only limited turnover in the initial phase of the product cycle. Floor-supported systems possess, thanks to the constant presence of the dealers during trading sessions, the special characteristic of liquidity, even in the case of small transactions, and thus ensure hedging efficiency. The greater flexibility on the one hand and the guarantee of adequate liquidity on the other could, at the start of EMU, prove to be a competitive advantage for the trading floor in introducing new products, compared with the futures markets where trading is completely electronic. For with a fully electronic trading system, such as Eurex, adjustments of both hardware and software must be made for product introductions and this is both time and cost intensive. If a contract specification is not accepted by market players, such investments of time and money are wasted and the corresponding amortisation irrecoverable. If one excludes the advantages of the trading floor in such test phases, however, then electronic trading will prove unbeatable in the processing of volume business.

## Success factor liquidity

Certainly, every futures exchange will abstain from increasing the competitive pressure on its existing products by introducing substitutes that could drain off liquidity from contracts already traded. A permanent coexistence of several contracts with the same maturity is unlikely in the world of the euro. The supply of liquidity for both the basis and hedging instruments may, after conversion to the euro, become the yardstick governing which interest rate futures are to be continued. On the assumption that the volatility of the yield spreads remains relatively low, the French Notionnel or the German Bund future may be suitable for hedging the price risks of Spanish government bonds. Hedging practices on the German Pfandbrief (mortgage bond) market are proof of this. As there is still no Pfandbrief future currently available on the DTB, the interest rate risks of Pfandbriefe are hedged with the aid of the futures contract on German federal medium-term notes, or Bundesobligationen (Bobl). Admittedly, the hedging quality provided by the Bobl for Pfandbriefe is not perfect. All the same, acceptance of the basis risk resulting from the incomplete correlation of the yields of Pfandbriefe and the Bobl is compensated by the advantage of higher liquidity in the Bobl market.

Both the high creditworthiness and the homogeneity of the underlying debt instruments of the German federal government and the adequate price volatility of the paper guarantee that the Bobl and Bund futures will be able to be used as hedging tools throughout the euro area. This is already beginning to happen. The Bund future contract, with 300,000 traded contracts daily, is clearly ahead of its French counterpart Notionnel, the daily traded volume of which is about 100,000. Even Bobl trading, with 120,000 contracts, is more intense than that of the French long-bond future. Moreover, the size of the market for German government bonds, with an outstanding volume of about Ecu700 billion, ensures an ample supply of material for delivery, and thereby excludes price manipulation resulting from large-volume transactions.

The competition for liquidity that could arise after denomination in euro is also a competition among public-sector issuers for market leadership in the euro bond market – whereby market leadership means pecuniary advantages for the issuer in the form of lower funding costs, and a guarantee, through the market-maker, of the highest possible liquidity supply. This means as a rule that the buying and selling prices hardly differ from each other, so that even large-volume transactions have no significant influence on prices, which enables the portfolio structure to be adapted swiftly to changed conditions on the international markets. With product and processing innovations on the German bond market for government issues and on the DTB geared to each other's needs, Germany's competitiveness as a financial centre and its government's standing as a benchmark issuer have been strengthened, helping the 10-year German federal bond to establish itself as the bond market leader in the euro area. In the contest for market share and thus for liquidity, the DTB and Matif at first suspended trading fees for both interest rate and equity products, as a result of which the DTB was able to regain a greater market share in Bund future business. In October 1997, the number of Bund future contracts traded by the DTB exceeded for the first time the volume traded on Liffe. Since then, the DTB has continuously expanded its lead through Bund future transactions so that by May 1998 its market share had reached 83 per cent.

## Europe's futures exchanges: cooperation or competition?

In the run-up to EMU, hectic activity has broken out on Europe's futures exchanges. Every decision is conditioned by the imminent monetary union, every individual futures exchange is preoccupied with the question of how to evaluate the chances of success for its product specifications and its competitive strategies. 1997 and 1998 are the years of positioning. During this time, the preconditions must be created for future participation by offering an attractive range of products and services for hedging and speculative transactions in US dollars, euros and yen across all time zones. This means pressure to cut operating costs, extend trading beyond normal hours and intensify development of efficient electronic trading systems. Competitive strategies based on new interest rate products, adjustments of contract specifications and lower fees generate only limited growth, so that the efforts of derivatives exchanges to secure higher liquidity are determined more and more by the optimisation of their clearing mechanisms, the provision of easier access to the futures markets for international market players and the faster formation of strategic alliances to exploit cross-border trading platforms.

With the merger of the DTB and Soffex – the Swiss futures exchange – to form Eurex in June 1998 and the cooperation agreement with France's Matif, the scene is set for the creation of a uniform euro area futures market that will establish new standards worldwide, in regard both to efficient and transparent clearing mechanisms and also to transaction costs and participation fees. Its fully electronic trading platform allowed the DTB to promote at an early stage the international marketability of its products through direct links to market players worldwide on the basis of so-called 'remote membership'. Meanwhile, there are almost 90 Eurex participants located outside of Germany and Switzerland, and their screens are to be found in all time zones so that 24-hour trading through Eurex products is now possible. This ensures a high degree of liquidity for the joint product range and improves the distribution channels. At the same time, through joint product development, the sharing of liquidity with new products is avoided.

The use of a uniform platform enables transaction prices and participation fees to be kept low, thus bringing another important advantage to Eurex, especially in comparison with floor-based trading systems. Whereas for the 'open outcry' systems a large staff of qualified personnel has to be employed to guarantee an efficient allocation of contract supply and demand – about 50,000 employees are engaged at the three derivatives exchanges in Chicago – in the case of electronic systems, hardly any variable costs are generated. Even advocates of floor trading concede that cost cuts of around 30 per cent can be achieved with the aid of a fully electronic system. Competitive prices, however, are what persuade market players to use the products and services of futures exchanges. And even electronic trading systems feel the pressure to limit the costs involved in modernising their software. The exploitation of synergies in the development of even more efficient systems may well act as a motive for intensified merger activity among futures exchanges in times to come.

The clearing structure chosen by Eurex points to the future. It offers market participants lower clearing costs and reduces their margin obligations through the consolidation of investments on the basis of net portfolios. Under the framework of Eurex, investors no longer have to fulfil margin requirements at a number of stock exchanges. This means that Eurex offers trading platforms and clearing 'from one hand'. Through the centralised security deposit, less liquidity is tied up; for investors, moreover, successful consolidation means both product diversity and a high degree of either hedging or performance. Furthermore, the Eurex clearing house has an essentially more diversified contract portfolio than either the DTB or Soffex. At the DTB interest rate transactions dominate with about 60 per cent, while the emphasis at Soffex is on share futures contracts, which represent about 70 per cent. At Eurex, interest rate contracts constitute 48 per cent, index contracts 32 per cent and share futures contracts 20 per cent. Thus the combined clearing house is safeguarded more strongly against disruptions in the individual cash market segments. Indeed, in the process of unifying cross-border trading platforms, it is fully conceivable that in order to limit their risk clearing houses will in future become responsible not only for financial futures but also for commodity transactions of all kinds.

## Market efficiency in the future

In view of the enormous potential for cost cutting offered by fully electronic trading systems, futures exchanges that still carry out their business in 'open outcry' will in the near future increasingly turn to computer-supported contract trading. Liffe already uses electronic systems after the day's floor-trading time, and from the end of 1999 the majority of its products will be tradable on electronic systems parallel to its traditional trading. Plans have also been announced for the US derivatives exchanges in Chicago to switch as soon as possible to electronic trading systems for their futures business. When these giants in the derivatives markets have converted to technically supported systems, there will be a strong case in favour of networking individual bourses into a global trading platform on which an optimum product range can be traded, furnished with a maximum supply of liquidity. Maximum liquidity means maximum efficiency in terms of prices and hence also hedging. Competition between contracts that satisfy the same hedging needs restricts, in principle, the efficiency of futures markets and has an adverse effect on transaction and clearing costs. The advantages that arise from a cooperative solution are already becoming clear with Eurex.

The increasing application of electronic systems to futures operations, which is currently observable and which is induced by competition, opens up additional chances for the derivatives exchanges. The market organisation of derivatives trading offers two decisive advantages over transactions with financial innovations that are traded outside the exchange. The first is that the clearing houses limit the risk of counterparty default, the second is that standardised products are traded. Admittedly, standardisation on the market for customised derivatives – the so-called OTC derivatives – continues to forge ahead, so that exchange trading in some of the OTC products is feasible. However, this presupposes significant development in terms of the electronic trading systems. These new systems must be even more efficiently designed in order to implement the more complex structure of OTC derivatives. Individual bourses are unlikely to be able to shoulder alone the high development and implementation costs for this new generation of trading systems. Thus not only will the trend towards cooperation and the merging of exchanges be intensified, but in future the alliances between futures exchanges and suppliers of information technology will also be closer.

# Appendix:
# Update of the 1997/98 BBA Credit Derivatives Survey

The global credit derivatives market had reached an estimated US$180 billion at the end of 1997. Projected growth rates for the credit derivatives market are extremely high: the London market is set to grow to US$380 billion by the end of the year 2000, while the global market is set to grow to US$740 billion.

London and New York continue to be the dominant centres, with most of the institutions surveyed stating that London had the largest market share. London was predicted to increase its market share by the year 2000, primarily due to its strategic position in the European time zone as the European secondary loan market develops.

Banks represent the largest buyers and sellers of credit protection using credit derivatives, currently accounting for about two-thirds of the buyers of credit protection, and a little over half of the sellers of credit protection. The dominance of the banking sector is expected to be somewhat eroded by the end of the year 2000 as a broader spectrum of firms enter the market, but banks are still expected to account for just over half the buyers of protection, and around 40 per cent of the sellers. Market professionals anticipate that the technical sophistication of insurance companies will lead them to rival securities firms as the second largest sellers of credit protection in the industry by the year 2000.

Credit default products (swaps and options) remain the most used credit derivative instrument, accounting for just over half of transactions at the end of 1997. This is expected to fall over the next two years as more firms begin to use the second generation products. Credit spread products in particular are expected to become more widely used, as banks and other financial firms look to protect themselves against movements in credit spreads, as opposed to specific credit events.

Our survey results indicate that credit derivatives will be increasingly written on corporate reference credits; the breadth of the corporate asset market, the search for higher returns and improvements in data on corporate assets were all cited as reasons for this predicted increase.

Credit derivatives are increasingly being written on loans, or loans and bonds combined, as opposed to bonds, and this trend is expected to continue. The size of the loan market, the better recovery rates on loans as opposed to bonds and an increased standardisation of loan transactions were seen as the principal reasons for this change.

The infrastructure of the market has been much improved. ISDA's recently published confirmation for non-sovereign over-the-counter credit swap transactions has been widely applauded. All of the interviewed institutions used the ISDA confirmation

**Exhibit A  Size of the credit derivatives market**

|  | 1997 | 1998 | 2000 |
|---|---|---|---|
| **Global market size (US$ billions)** | **180** | **350** | **740** |
| London market size (US$ billions) | 70 | 170 | 380 |
| London's percentage of the global market (%) | 39 | 49 | 51 |

*Source:* 1997/98 BBA Credit Derivatives Survey.

**Exhibit B  Structure of the credit derivatives market (%)**

|  | 1997 | 2000 |
|---|---|---|
| Banks' share of protection buyers' market | 64 | 51 |
| Securities houses' share of protection buyers' market | 18 | 15 |
| Banks' share of protection sellers' market | 54 | 43 |
| Securities houses' share of protection sellers' market | 22 | 19 |
| Market share of credit default products | 52 | 38 |
| Market share of credit spread products | 13 | 21 |
| Market share of sovereign assets | 35 | 29 |
| Market share of corporate assets | 35 | 44 |
| Percentage of bond-based transactions | 53 | 29 |
| Percentage of loan-based transactions | 30 | 36 |

*Source:* 1997/98 BBA Credit Derivatives Survey.

as a template for their credit swap documentation, which in some cases amounted to as much as 80 per cent of their total credit derivative transactions. Also, consultation between banks, trade associations, and regulators has recently produced new regulatory guidance for credit derivatives in both Europe and North America that rewards prudent credit risk management.

But more remains to be done. Despite the new ISDA confirmation, surveyed institutions still cited a lack of standard documentation, along with regulatory environment and market liquidity, as the largest constraints to the growth of the credit derivatives market.

Perhaps the greatest development since the first BBA survey has been the proving of the market in action. The Asian crisis brought credit derivatives to the fore in late 1997 and allowed the market to demonstrate its maturity and worth. At times, credit derivatives proved to be more liquid than the underlying assets.

# The co-publishers

# Credit Derivatives at Barclays Capital

Barclays Capital is the investment banking division of Barclays PLC, one of the largest multinational financial services groups in the world. Barclays Capital offers a full range of derivatives products and has formed a special unit to provide credit and emerging market derivatives.

As part of the Barclays group, Barclays Capital has access to the balance sheet of Barclays Bank PLC, an institution with assets of some £235 billion, capital resources of almost £11 billion and a AA credit rating. Headquartered in London, Barclays Capital operates in all the world's major financial centres and maintains offices in 16 cities around the globe. The firm made operating profits of £248 million and £201 million in 1997 and 1996, respectively.

Barclays Capital provides its clients with a broad range of integrated international debt, lending and risk management products. Its core businesses include debt capital markets, syndicated loans, structured and project finance, structured capital markets, derivatives, foreign exchange, money markets, futures, commodities and private equity. The firm serves governments, supranational organisations, corporates, banks, insurance companies and other institutional investors.

As a leading participant in the global markets, Barclays Capital's debt capital markets operation is consistently ranked first in sterling Eurobond issuance, and its syndicated loan business is ranked first in Europe. The firm's structured and project finance business is one of the world's foremost franchises. Its private equity operation has invested in nearly 300 businesses in transactions ranging in size from £10 million to more than £250 million.

Barclays Capital has been instrumental in the internationalisation of the sterling market, bringing to the market first-time sterling issuers such as the World Bank, Fannie Mae, Colombia and the United Mexican States. The firm has successfully built on its sterling franchise to become a significant player in other market segments, including floating rate notes, Deutschmarks, US dollars, yen and euros. The firm is extremely active in the trading of UK gilts and Japanese government bonds, and it was recently awarded primary government bond dealer status in France and South Africa.

## The Global Derivatives Group

Barclays Capital's derivatives capability spans all products and serves the firm's entire client base, including commercial and investment banks, insurers, investment funds and corporates. The firm provides derivative products across all asset classes, and its derivatives business is especially active in government bond markets and key emerging markets across the globe.

Barclays Capital's Global Derivatives Group provides generic and structured derivative products linked to the international fixed income, commodity and equity markets. The group excels in providing integrated risk management solutions for international fixed income issuers and investors. Using state-of-the-art analytics and expert derivatives teams posted around the globe, the group designs risk management solutions across all asset classes to meet the transaction and portfolio needs of clients.

Supported by Barclays Capital's global securities research and trading operations, the Global Derivatives Group can price, structure and execute fully customised derivatives trades with the timeliness that global markets demand. The group's risk management expertise is anchored by Barclays Bank's financial strength and AA credit rating, making Barclays Capital a particularly secure counterparty for all derivatives transactions.

Barclays' Global Derivatives Group provides investment and risk management services in five major product areas:

*Interest rate derivatives.* The Global Derivatives Group offers the full spectrum of interest rate swaps, forwards and options. The group uses the most innovative derivatives technologies to create customised hedging, trading and financing strategies for fixed income issuers and investors.

*Currency derivatives.* The Global Derivatives Group provides the widest range of foreign exchange derivative instruments in over 30 currencies. Teams of FX professionals based in New York, London, Paris, Hong Kong and Tokyo provide continuous market coverage and 24-hour execution across all time zones.

*Equity derivatives.* Supported by Barclays Capital's global trading and research operations, the Global Derivatives Group offers swaps, options and structured investments for equity issues listed around the world.

*Credit derivatives.* Barclays has built one of the first global credit derivatives operations to integrate all fixed income asset classes, including public and non-public debt, commercial loans and high-yield and emerging market bonds. This capability allows Barclays to design customised derivatives strategies that integrate all risk parameters for all major fixed income markets and asset classes to meet the precise risk profiles and market views of clients.

*Emerging market derivatives.* The Global Derivatives Group executes a wide range of derivatives transactions for the emerging debt markets of Asia, Latin America, Eastern Europe and Africa. The group offers in-depth research and fully integrated trading and derivatives execution for over 45 emerging debt markets.

## Global Asset Derivatives

Barclays' Global Asset Derivatives team, a division of the Global Derivatives Group, specialises in the design and application of credit and emerging market derivatives.

This team creates customised derivatives that isolate and trade the credit risk of public and non-public securities and loans, allowing clients to manage risks prudently and optimise portfolio performance. The Global Asset Derivatives team has created a proprietary risk modelling system that precisely measures the credit risk of single securities and whole portfolios. This system allows Barclays to design integrated derivatives solutions that both control risk and extract new value from credit-sensitive securities, loans and portfolios.

The Global Asset Derivatives team can provide credit derivatives for all credit-sensitive asset classes. In the US fixed income market alone, Barclays can use credit derivatives to hedge risks, unlock embedded value and restructure investment profiles for over 2,500 credit issues, including high-yield bonds, asset-backed securities and CBOs.

In the emerging debt markets of Asia, Latin America, Eastern Europe and Africa, the unit can design derivatives packages that manage the complex dynamics of credit, interest rate, sovereign and currency risks to meet the risk profiles and market views of clients. Barclays Capital's global trading network and extensive research capabilities provide exceptional flexibility to structure and execute derivatives trades and strategies in over 35 emerging markets, including some 25 local currency markets.

The team offers products based on a wide range of underlying assets and indices, including:

- corporate bonds
- corporate loans
- CBOs and asset-backed securities
- non-G24 government bonds
- emerging market bonds and credit indices
- mutual funds
- trade receivables and trade paper
- interest rate and inflation indices
- synthetic credit/equity instruments

The team can design derivatives packages for a wide range of applications, including:

*Investment management.* Investors and risk managers can use derivatives to enhance their returns or to tailor the risk profiles of individual securities or entire portfolios to suit their investment goals and risk tolerances. For example, clients may purchase principal-indexed notes with tailored maturities that are linked to the performance of bond indices or local currencies and that also guarantee a minimum principal redemption of 50 per cent. Or they may buy leveraged investment vehicles to gain exposure to the performance of baskets of bonds or currencies that can yield a multiple of the total return on the underlying securities.

*Market access.* Derivatives can be used to provide efficient access to markets with local restrictions and high transaction costs. In these markets, using derivatives to create synthetic securities can be far more efficient and far more flexible than buying and selling securities directly on the cash market. This is particularly true of local currency and other markets where direct access is restricted. Barclays' Global Asset Derivatives team offers local currency-linked products on a currency-hedged or unhedged basis. These instruments can be linked to corporate and government bonds, loans, deposit rates or local currency exchange rates.

*Diversification.* Derivatives allow investors to customise fixed income securities and exposures by maturity, currency, investment structure and leverage. This flexibility promotes portfolio diversification by greatly expanding the range of global credits available to portfolio managers. For example, credit derivatives can be used to create synthetic exposures to specific corporate credits for maturities that do not exist in the cash market.

*Risk management.* Derivatives allow investors to manage and trade the risk elements of individual securities or entire portfolios, including default, credit spread, duration and liquidity risks. The flexibility of derivatives technology allows investment managers to hedge some risks and assume other risks to meet precise investment mandates and market views. Risk management products range from simple total return swaps to complex hybrid structures such as credit default protection derivatives packages linked to commodity prices.

The Global Asset Derivatives team has designed derivatives solutions for a wide range of institutions, investors and corporations. The unit's principal clients fall into four groups:

Retail institutions such as mutual funds, S&Ls and private banks use asset derivatives to create yield-enhanced fixed income products.

Pension funds and insurers employ asset derivatives to manage duration risk in their fixed income portfolios.

Commercial and investment banks use asset derivatives to manage the credit and market exposures of their loan and bond portfolios.

Corporate treasuries use asset derivatives to manage their assets and liabilities.

## Further information

For more information, please contact:

| | | |
|---|---|---|
| Jane Herring | (London) | Tel: (44) 171 773 9844 |
| Jess Saypoff | (New York) | Tel: (1) 212 412 2900 |
| Gary Wang | (Hong Kong) | Tel: (852) 2903 2860 |

# A brief portrait

**Helaba
Landesbank Hessen-Thüringen
Girozentrale, Frankfurt am Main / Erfurt**

With effect from 1 July 1992, the Bank was
renamed "Landesbank Hessen-Thüringen".
On that date, the Treaty on the Formation of
a Joint Savings Banks Organisation between
the federal states of Hesse and Thuringia
came into force.

## Historic roots

The origins of the Bank can be traced back to
the early 19th century. The former Hessische
Landesbank was formed in 1953 by the merger
of Hessische Landesbank Darmstadt (founded
1940), Nassauische Landesbank Wiesbaden
(founded 1840) as well as of Landeskreditkasse
zu Kassel (founded 1832).

## Worldwide presence

Today, the Bank has two head offices – in Frankfurt am Main and Erfurt. In addition, Helaba has branches and representative offices in Darmstadt, Kassel, Düsseldorf, Stuttgart and Berlin. At international level it maintains branch offices, subsidiaries and representative offices in the financial centres London, New York, Luxembourg, Zurich, Amsterdam and Dublin. It is also present in Paris, Brussels, Budapest, Hong Kong, Madrid, Prague and Warsaw.

## Legal form and owner

Helaba is a legal entity under public law. The owner and guarantor of the Bank is the Savings Bank and Giro Association Hesse-Thuringia (Sparkassen- und Giroverband Hessen-Thüringen – SGVHT), a joint institution of the municipal savings banks and their guarantors in Hesse and Thuringia. State supervision of the Bank and the Association is exercised by the Ministries for Economics and Finance in Hesse and Thuringia in their capacity as general supervisory authority for the savings banks. Executive bodies of the Bank are the Board of Guarantors, the Supervisory Board and the Board of Managing Directors.

Helaba has for many years ranked among the banks which have received an AAA rating from the three major rating agencies for their unsecured long-term liabilities.

## A bank with a public mandate

As one of the leading state and municipal banks in Germany, Helaba lends its support in many ways to economic and structural measures in its core business regions of Hesse and Thuringia. Thus the Land Trust Agency (Landestreuhand-stelle Hessen – LTH), an independent division of the Bank, assists in the realisation of public development activities in Hesse. In the Free State of Thuringia, the Bank holds shares in Mittelständische Beteiligungsgesellschaft (MBG, a finance company providing equity capital to small and medium-sized companies) and in Bürgschaftsbank Thüringen (BBT – a guarantee bank). In Erfurt, the Bank operates a Euro Info Centre by virtue of an official mandate of the European Commission, in addition to its banking activities.

Helaba provides advisory services and support to the federal government, the federal states and municipalities with regard to the planning, financing and realisation of their investment plans. In addition to the traditional municipal loan and the issue of bonds and notes, the Bank offers its public authority customers special financing possibilities such as project and asset finance.

## Partner of the savings banks

Helaba exercises the function of a central bank for the Hessian and Thuringian savings banks. Within the S-Finanzgruppe Hessen-Thüringen, the savings banks occupy a particular position; they are customers, owners and partners of the Bank. For this purpose, the range of products and services offered by the Bank is being further developed, in line with requirements. It is the aim of Helaba to provide expertise and services for the savings banks to strengthen and support their strategic and competitive position.

## Customer- and market-oriented universal bank

As a universal bank, Helaba concentrates on wholesale business. At both domestic and international level, it co-operates with large corporations, institutional investors, high net-worth private investors and governmental institutions. In this respect, Helaba concentrates on the business areas Financing, Real Estate Business, Asset Management, Treasury and Sales, Transactions and Services as well as Specialised Business (building saving and trustee business). For the entire range of products offered by the Bank, relationship managers have been appointed in the segments Savings Banks, Large Corporations, Companies, Municipal Corporations and Institutional Investors.

## Capital markets division

Helaba's Debt Capital Markets Division was established in 1994 to promote the Bank's fixed income business. Its main focus is on structuring primary and trading secondary market debt products. Capital Markets' activities consist of origination, asset trading and a comprehensive syndicate group.

Origination comprises structuring and acquisition of loans and bonds as straight, structured and repackaged issues. The choice of issuers is rooted in the Bank's key account customer system and adds to an overall customer service. Asset trading spans the full spectrum of debt products. It has gained market reputation especially with its successful asset swap trading and German corporate debt activities. The division's strategy is rigidly kept customer oriented: no transaction will be realised without a link to clients' needs.

Since the beginning of last year the team has been involved in Credit Derivatives. This positive attitude towards the new tool is based on the view that Credit Derivatives will rapidly continue to attract a great deal of attention abroad as well as in Germany. The new product range will provide a flexible set of alternatives within structuring and risk management procedures.

# GLOBAL RISK MANAGEMENT SOLUTIONS
# FROM PRICEWATERHOUSECOOPERS

**"We view risk not as a liability, but, when properly managed, as a powerful asset that can bestow competitive advantage on the organisation that is committed to managing risk at a strategic and tactical level."**

*In a global business environment where success increasingly requires the rapid application of knowledge to address complex issues, PricewaterhouseCoopers can call on around 140,000 of the best minds in the world to help our clients succeed.*

*Deregulation, privatisation, emerging markets and quantum improvements in telecommunications and information technology have radically altered today's business landscape, creating these issues and challenging chief executives.*

*Through our Global Risk Management Solutions we help clients to identify the potential risks associated with such challenges, and to maximise the opportunities they can produce when correctly managed.*

*Our global organisation and presence allows our professionals to approach risk management from an enterprise wide perspective, regardless of size or geographic diversity. Combined with the depth of our risk management expertise, this sophisticated and integrated approach to risk management and control allows Global Risk Management Solutions to bring our clients the ability to confidently integrate risk management into their strategic business planning.*

*Our industry experts operate within a framework of five service areas:*

- *Strategic Risk Management*

- *Operational and Systems Risk Management*

- *Compliance Risk Management*

- *Internal Audit Services*

- *Financial Risk Management*

*www.pwcglobal.com*

# GLOBAL RISK

# MANAGEMENT

# SOLUTIONS

PricewaterhouseCoopers Global Risk Management Solutions practice has around 5,000 professional staff worldwide offering an integrated approach to risk management which helps businesses around the world to identify, measure, monitor, manage and improve their strategic, financial and operational risk management and control processes.

**P**RICE**W**ATERHOUSE**C**OOPERS

www.pwcglobal.com

PricewaterhouseCoopers refers to the UK firm of PricewaterhouseCoopers and to other members of the worldwide PricewaterhouseCoopers organisation.

## Strategic Risk Management

Working with senior managers, our professionals in the field of Strategic Risk Management help businesses identify, assess, manage and monitor the risks facing their organisations as they strive to achieve their goals. We have established a highly effective approach for facilitating risk assessments with our clients across a wide range of industries and countries.

## Operational and Systems Risk Management

As business processes become increasingly sophisticated and transactions are conducted at greater speed, the role of technology in servicing the relationship between supplier and customer increases – and with it the possibility of risk. We assist clients with identifying, assessing, managing and monitoring such risks at the business unit, process or functional level through a range of services focusing on:

- Controls & Assurance Services – focusing on the design and implementation of controls for organisations undertaking major change projects and the provision of independent controls assurance to confirm that controls are operating as intended.

- Operational Risk Services – focusing on the risks associated with ongoing business operations and major change initiatives, including business continuity planning, operational risk, financial process review services, contractor compliance and IT value management.

- Technology Risk Services.

- Deployment Services.

- Environmental Services – focusing on helping businesses to understand and maximise the impact of environmental issues on their organisations.

## Compliance Risk Management

Working with clients, we assist them with managing the risk of non-compliance with internal and external laws, regulations and policies.

## Internal Audit Services

We provide clients with an objective look at their organisations, providing an evaluation of internal audit unit performance against professional standards and peer organisations. We can identify areas for improvement and develop action plans, while our Internal Audit Advisory Services can assist clients in developing new audit functions, re-engineering existing functions or benchmarking audit functions against other world-class audit organisations.

www.pwcglobal.com

## Financial Risk Management

*With the largest financial risk management practice in the world, PricewaterhouseCoopers is the leader in developing and evaluating in-house risk management capabilities.*

*Our professionals have extensive experience in managing risk for financial institutions, corporate and energy markets. Their backgrounds vary from top management positions in leading financial institutions, energy companies or corporate treasuries to front and back office positions in financial institutions and other corporations. In addition, we have a strong group of quantitative professionals and business analysts.*

*Together, they help clients to manage risk at the financial level, including all types of market risks, liquidity and credit risks.*

*We provide risk frameworks that include a definition of risk appetite, management decision processes, systems, measures and controls, organisation, policy and management reporting. Our approach also includes ways to measure risk-adjusted return on capital and to link performance evaluation to the creation of shareholder value.*

***Market Risk.*** *For market risk in the areas of capital markets and derivatives, we assess and develop Value at Risk methodologies, perform model reviews of derivative valuations, and build risk management organisations, limit structures and policies. We not only support standard industry methodologies such as RiskMetrics™ and CreditMetrics™ but also develop our own methodologies to address our clients' risk management issues.*

***Credit Risk.*** *Further, the explosion in issuer volume, credit derivatives and the liquidity of credit products has propelled banks and securities firms beyond traditional credit approvals and towards active portfolio credit risk measurement and management. We help clients develop portfolio level exposure measures, portfolio management tools to assess concentration/ diversification, and the organisational processes that create profitable and risk-efficient portfolios.*

***Technology as a Risk Management Tool.*** *Firms rely on technology to help them manage financial risk on both a transaction and a portfolio basis. Determining what technology to use is just the beginning. We can help clients select the right technology, implement it, adapt it to their specific needs and integrate it with their existing systems.*

***Risk-Adjusted Performance Measurement.*** *We focus on risk adjusted performance measures to maximise shareholder value, and we can calibrate and build measurement methodologies, and performance measurement systems (and the related management processes) to link risk to shareholder value.*

*For more information on how Global Risk Management Solutions from PricewaterhouseCoopers can add value to your business, visit our website.*

*www.pwcglobal.com*